D1055273

GAUGUIN

GAUGUIN

GEORGES BOUDAILLE

759.4
GAU

TUDOR PUBLISHING COMPANY

NEW YORK

LIBRARY
SOUTHERN UNION STATE JUNIOR COLLEGE
WADLEY ALABAMA

TRANSLATED FROM THE FRENCH
BY ALISA JAFFA

© 1964 EDITIONS AIMERY SOMOGY PARIS

Printed and bound in the Netherlands

FOREWORD

PAUL GAUGUIN, like Van Gogh and Cézanne, was one of the fore-runners of modern painting. All three introduced previously unex-pressed emotions into art, developed a new freedom, and entirely changed the concept of the beautiful. After them, painting could not return to what it had been in the nineteenth century without seeming lifeless, insignificant and outdated.

Gauguin heightened the expressive value of line, developed the emotional power of colour, and introduced a new concept of space into painting, which differed from classical perspective, thus opening up new avenues to later generations of artists. His contribution is so important that in his time he seemed revolutionary and outraged the sensibilities of his contemporaries. As often happens, it was not until after his death that the value of his works was finally acknow-ledged. The paintings which he had sold for trifling sums during his lifetime subsequently soared in price and today are bought for astro-nomical figures by the largest museums and the richest collectors in the world.

Like Van Gogh, whose path crossed Gauguin's at one point, he led a passionate, tormented and at times dramatic existence, a source of fascination to many. But the romantic aspect of his life should not be allowed to overshadow his work. The life of great artists is only of interest to us because of the moment of genius they displayed. Had they left no work for posterity, no matter how romantic their lives, they would long since have been forgotten. The events of Gauguin's life, his pangs of conscience, his inner conflicts, and his public disputes, only interest us in so far as they help us to reach a better understanding of the man, and thereby of his work.

In this volume we shall attempt to show how Gauguin's painting and the events in his life interacted. Sometimes his idea of the creative work that lay ahead of him compelled Gauguin to abandon the way of life he was leading at the time; sometimes, conversely, his professional and emotional life affected his painting and modified it.

Although the facts are well-known, a broad outline of Gauguin's life should not make the subject any less interesting. By dividing it into four main parts, each of them marking a stage in the liberation of the man and the victory of the artist, we hope to contribute to a better understanding of this unique life story.

The first stage, the childhood spent in Peru, followed by service in the marines, marriage, family, social success, and then the renunciation of all this, his meeting with Pissarro, and finally the break with his wife, Mette, are the formative years, the years of awakening. Gauguin's background was a curious one and his early years were in no sense ordinary. The potential originality was already there. Believing himself to be no different from other men, and having in fact done everything in his power to become like them, he gradually became aware that this was impossible for him, and that he was made for other things. He felt compelled to break with everything that was holding him back, and suddenly found himself alone in Paris in 1885 in the most abject poverty.

From 1885 to 1891 he was as unsettled in his art as he was in his life. He made friends only to quarrel with the majority of them, travelled, stayed in Brittany, went off on a crazy escapade to Panama and Martinique, returned to Paris, where he became friendly with the poets of the day, and met with so many disappointments that he became thoroughly disillusioned and decided to run away from Europe, society and civilization. These years of wandering were not wasted years. Gauguin had learned a great deal about life and about art. He had not yet found himself and his own truth, but he now knew what he was not, and when he left for Tahiti in 1891 he was going in pursuit of himself and of a universe that he was to make his own through the magic of his painting.

Gauguin remained in Tahiti from 1891 to 1893, and then returned again from 1895 to 1903, though, strictly speaking, the last two years of his life were spent on the Marquesas Islands. These periods in Tahiti were the two greatest chapters in this extraordinary life – a life that by ordinary human standards was a failure, but which produced some of the most original works of the time.

Some readers may wonder why I have dwelt at such length on the importance of some ten or twelve years in the life of an artist, who began to draw at the age of twenty-three. Obviously, the Tahitian period is not the whole of Gauguin's painting; there are numerous Impressionist works, and the important period in Brittany, exemplified by such masterpieces as *The Yellow Christ* (page 104) and *Vision after the Sermon* (page 49). But if Gauguin's work had consisted only of these earlier paintings, and he had never gone to Tahiti, his work would not have gained the stature that it has in the history of modern art. It seems that Gauguin sought to dissociate himself in every way from his former existence, in order to find the conditions most conducive to creativity, only to find himself in a desperate and hostile situation. When at last he was on his own, and virtually abandoned, he showed that he had the ability to bring to life the intense, mystical and sensual painting he had dreamed of. Thus the great Tahiti works have somewhat belatedly been acknowledged as the justification of the artist's faults, his errors and his ravings.

In the realm of art, genius justifies all, and as the example of Gauguin shows, genius is the fruit borne of infinite patience.

When does an artist's life begin? On the day he produces his first work? This would seem logical, if one were simply concerned with the artist, and not with the man. Indeed, why not the date of the first public showing of one of his works? But official dates do not explain the origin of the artist, who must have come from somewhere. Thus we find ourselves going back into his genealogy, and where there is a family history it is difficult to know at which point to break off this investigation of the past.

Gauguin began to draw seriously in 1871; he exhibited at the Salon for the first time in 1876; these facts are comparatively unimportant. More significant by far was his meeting with Camille Pissarro in 1876. He was born in June 1848, at the height of a political crisis, when the Second Republic, which had only just been proclaimed, was about to yield to its President, Bonaparte. A few days later, when the new government had failed to keep its promises and disbanded the newly instituted national industrial units, fifty thousand workers manned the barricades and there was fighting in Paris. From the very first days of his life, the young Paul Gauguin was surrounded by an atmosphere of extreme unrest.

Because his grandparents, and their parents too, had been unlike other people, before he ever saw the light of day Paul Gauguin had little chance of being a man like other men, or of ending his days as a sober-minded official or an inoffensive clerk. His father, Clovis Gauguin, impelled by worthy Republican sentiments, worked without incident as a journalist on the *National*, but his mother, whose maiden name was Aline Chazal, was to give him a heritage that was far from ordinary. At the time of Gauguin's birth, his maternal grand-father, André Chazal, was serving a prison sentence for the attempted murder of his wife, the famous revolutionary propagandist, Flora Tristan, who had died four years earlier in 1844. It may well have been jealousy, understandable in a deserted husband, that drove André Chazal in a moment of uncontrolled passion to commit this act of violence. The case of Flora Tristan is far more complex. André

METTE GAUGUIN AND HER SON JEAN. 1881.
Private Collection, Nantes.

Chazal came from a family with no history; his father was teacher of drawing at the Natural History Museum. The family of Tristan Morosco, on the other hand, had a remarkable history and played an active and important part in Paul Gauguin's own life.

Flora Tristan was the daughter of Marie-Thérèse Laisney and Don Mariano de Tristan Morosco. Little is known about Gauguin's great-grandmother. She belonged to a group of refugee French Royalists in Spain during the Revolution of 1789. In Bilbao she made the acquaintance of a Spanish colonel in the Dragoons, and went to live with him. In 1802 the couple went to settle in France. Don Mariano bought the 'Petit Château', a large residence on the Grande rue de Vaugirard, where his mistress bore him first a girl, Flora, and then a boy, but still refused to marry him. Shortly after his death in 1807, all Spanish property in France was seized by the government of Napoleon, then at war with Spain, and, despite lengthy court proceedings, Marie-Thérèse Laisney lost all her possessions. She had a difficult life, and nourished her daughter with memories of her noble father, whom she said was descended from the Aztec king, Montezuma. Gauguin was later to refer to his Indian blood.

It was not so much love as a desire to escape poverty that led the eighteen-year-old Flora to marry a lithographic printer, André Chazal. Flora, who was ambitious and impatient, found her husband's mediocrity hard to bear, and things went badly. She left her first two children with her mother, and in 1825 ran away, while she was pregnant with another daughter, Aline – Gauguin's future mother.

Flora Tristan devoted much of her life to writing about the proletariat and to the fight for workers' liberties. When she learned that her father's younger brother, Don Pio, had taken part in the Peruvian war of independence, she wrote to him, demanding her share of the inheritance, and received a legacy worth three thousand hard piastres and an income. She seduced a sea-captain by the name of Chabrier, and set off for Peru in order to claim the whole of her inheritance. To no avail. In 1838 she published an account of the journey under the title of *Pérégrinations d'une Paria* (Peregrinations of a Pariah), and became an exponent of the theories of Saint-Simon.

In 1835 a particularly painful episode occurred. André Chazal, who had gone from bad to worse, had managed to take little Aline, now a girl of twelve, away from her mother, and attempted to seduce her. She ran away and returned to her mother. André Chazal was thrown in prison, and Flora obtained a legal separation. On 10th September 1838 André Chazal waited for Flora outside her house, and shot her in the chest. The trial created a tremendous stir. Flora Tristan was now famous, and contributed to various newspapers, wrote a novel called *Memphis ou le Prolétaire* (Memphis or the Proletarian), and campaigned for the reintroduction of divorce, which had been suppressed since 1816. Flora had meanwhile been given permission to drop the name Chazal and resume her maiden name of Tristan. In her *Promenades à Londres* (Walks through London), written in 1840, she described the poverty of the English proletariat. In 1843 she published *L'union ouvrière* (The Trade Union), continued to campaign militantly, and in 1844 she went on a propaganda and lecture tour throughout France, gravely weakening her health. She died of a stroke on 14th November 1844 at Bordeaux. Such was Gauguin's grandmother. He was to write of her: 'My grandmother was an odd sort of woman. She was called Flora Tristan. Proudhon said that she was a genius. I know nothing about it myself, and I am prepared to believe him.'

Her daughter Aline married Clovis Gauguin two years later, in 1846. In 1847 Fernande-Marcelline-Marie was born, and Paul a year later. Meanwhile French workers opened a national subscription fund, and erected a monument to their heroine, Flora Tristan, in the Bordeaux cemetery.

Today there is a modest plaque on 52 rue Notre-Dame de Lorette, telling the passer-by that this was where the artist was born.

SPANISH — HIS MOTHER-TONGUE

On 10th December 1848 Louis-Napoleon Bonaparte was elected President of the Republic. From a political and social point of view Gauguin's parents would not have been directly concerned by the

HOUSE IN THE COUNTRY. 1874.
Spreiregen Collection.

turn of events, had it not been for the fact that his father was on the editorial staff of the *National*, which had been campaigning against the candidature of the new President. Clovis Gauguin was apprehensive, even though he was not one of the leading figures involved and consequently not in immediate danger. After the rue Transnonain affair, which had inspired a dramatic lithograph by Daumier, he decided to leave the country immediately, rather than await imprisonment or exile. Aline, his wife, recalled her mother's accounts of the wealthy Tristan Morosco family. In Peru they might find relatives, and even a lavish welcome. Clovis Gauguin's dream was to find financial backing and found a newspaper in Lima.

In August 1849 the family set sail from Le Havre on the 'Albert'. Travelling conditions were quite deplorable. The captain was a brutal tyrant who forced his passengers to follow a routine that was anything but restful. The endless wrangling affected the health of Clovis Gauguin, who was already suffering from a weak heart. He died suddenly as the boat put in at Port-Famine, today called Punta Arenas, at the tip of Patagonia, and was buried there.

Aline Gauguin now found herself in an appalling situation, compelled to complete this hazardous journey alone with two small children. Paul and his sister were doubtless too young to appreciate the agonies and mishaps of this voyage, but one cannot help feeling that their early years must have been deeply affected by the distressing experiences suffered by their mother. In retrospect patterns emerge, and it is tempting to see a fateful streak in Paul Gauguin's destiny which drove him fifty years later to meet his death, like his father, at another 'end of the world', in the solitude of the Marquesas Islands.

On her arrival in Peru, all the fears and anxieties of Aline Gauguin were dispelled. Her great-uncle, Don Pio, who was already over a hundred years old (he was born in 1743 and did not die until 1856), accorded her an unexpectedly affectionate welcome, giving the lie to all the accounts of her mother, Flora Tristan. Admittedly, the circumstances were different. Flora had come to demand an inheritance which she considered as her rightful due, whereas Aline came as a poor, tearful widow with two dependent children, pleading for hospitality. Meanwhile the wealth of the Tristan Moroscos had increased even further and the family was now among the most influential in Peru. Don Pio, who had been unsuccessful in his attempts to become President of the Republic, had revenged himself by having one of his sons-in-law elected, Don José Rufino Echenique.

Aline and her children, Paul and Marie, were to benefit from this incredible wealth – a residence as large as a castle, innumerable domestic staff, luxury and comfort, all this existing side by side with the poverty of the common people. This colonial type of society was to be the background of Paul's life until he was seven years old. For all its medieval structure, that held the people vigorously in check,

LAKE IN THE PLAIN. 1873.
Fitzwilliam Museum, Cambridge.

Peru was a country undergoing radical changes, a prey to internal conflicts, family rivalries and personal ambitions.

It is difficult to form an accurate picture of Paul Gauguin's life during this period. There is no doubt that vivid memories of it remained with him, leaving strange and occasionally morbid impressions, mingling with his taste for luxury and the exotic, and an already awakened sensuality. But we are obliged to keep to the known facts, and leave any embellishments to Gauguin. Many years later he wrote a collection of personal memories and essays assembled under the title of *Avant et Après*, which he sent to André Fontainas in 1903 from the Marquesas Islands, a few months before his death, in the hope of having them published in book form. Here he says: 'I have a strangely visual memory, and I can recall this period, and our house and a whole lot of incidents, the monument in the President's house, and the church with the carved wooden dome that was put on afterwards.

'I can still see our little negress, whose duty it was to carry to the church the small carpet, which was used as a kneeling mat. I can also see our Chinese servant, who was so good at ironing the laundry. It was he who found me in a grocer's shop, sitting between two casks of molasses, sucking at some sugar-cane when my poor mother had frantically sent everyone out to search for me. I've always had this craze for running away, for when I was nine, in Orleans, I decided to run away to the forest of Bondy, with a handkerchief filled with sand tied to the end of a stick, which I carried over my shoulder. For me this picture had become irresistible – the traveller with his little bundle and stick over his shoulder . . .

'Four years went by, when one fine day urgent letters arrived from France, insisting on my mother's return in order to arrange the details of my maternal grandfather's estate. My mother, who was so in-experienced in business matters, went back to France, to Orleans. This proved to be a mistake, for in the following year, 1856, her old uncle, who had been dallying with death for so long, finally died.

AUTUMN LANDSCAPE. 1871.
Einar Dessau Collection, Copenhagen.

'Don Pio de Tristan y Morosco was no more. He had lived a hundred and thirteen years. In memory of his dearly-loved brother, he had settled an income on my mother of five thousand hard piastres, which came to a little over twenty-five thousand francs. When he was on his deathbed the family made the old man change his will, and seized hold of this immense fortune, which was all squandered in a wild spending spree in Paris. The only cousin who stayed behind remained tremendously rich, and still lives today in the form of a mummy. Peru is famous for its mummies.

'The following year Echenique came to my mother to try and come to some arrangement, and my mother, ever proud, replied: "All or nothing!" So it was nothing.'

The most significant feature of his years in Peru is, however, that in his youth he had the opportunity of seeing around him vases and statuettes, dating from the pre-Columbian period. He may only have retained a faint impression of them, but once again in his mother's house he could see pieces that she had brought back from Peru, and he was to be most upset when years later they disappeared in the fire that destroyed his house at Saint-Cloud in 1870. These Peruvian objects were to arouse in him a fascination for primitive art, so that, unlike many of his contemporaries, he never found it shocking; on the contrary it claimed his attention as the expression of beliefs and aspirations of peoples that he refused to regard as inferior.

SCHOOLDAYS AND APPRENTICESHIP

There were two factors that influenced Aline Gauguin in her decision to return to France with her two children. In Orleans grandfather Guillaume Gauguin, who was now nearing seventy, felt that he was an old man and would like to see his grandchildren again before he died. He had made his will, and shared his possessions between the children of his son, Clovis, and his other son, Isidore. He wrote insistently. Moreover, in Peru things looked bad: General Castilla, leader of the opposition, had started a civil war. He marched on Lima, seeking to overthrow President Echenique, son-in-law of Don Pio.

Don Pio's legacy would have been far more important than that of grandfather Gauguin. But Aline, taking fright, or simply feeling homesick for France, embarked for Le Havre just before General Castilla entered Lima, and arrived in Orleans with her children shortly after Guillaume Gauguin died. They were taken in by Uncle Isidore, who was known as 'Zizi'. The atmosphere was far from gay. Isidore Gauguin had been deported to North Africa for having demonstrated against the coup d'état of 2nd December, but with the greater leniency that followed, he had been allowed to return to Orleans, where he was kept under house arrest.

For the young Paul Gauguin the enormous change in his surroundings was unsettling; having never spoken any language other than Spanish, he could barely understand his playmates and his teachers, and he had to adapt himself to the unaccustomed bleak and cold climate. First he attended a boarding school in Orleans as a day-boy, and then, when his mother went to Paris to set up as a dressmaker, he went as a boarder to a small secondary school.

Paul Gauguin was a difficult child, reserved and quick-tempered, who worked badly in class. He was already dreaming of distant horizons, and when it came to choosing a career, he announced that he wished to be a sailor. He apparently wanted to get away from this environment, in which he had found it so hard to settle down. There was talk of the Naval College, but Paul was not a good enough scholar and in 1865 he was in any case already too old to sit for the entrance examination. It was as an ordinary apprentice that he set sail on the 'Luzitano', a three-masted ship of six hundred and fifty-four tons (not one thousand, two hundred, as he was to claim later). The apprenticeship led to the rank of naval officer.

On the quayside of Le Havre, Paul Gauguin was overcome by a wave of excitement such as he had not known for a long time. A new life stretched out ahead of him. He was a man. His amorous life began with a visit to some brothel in the harbour area, and his predecessor on the boat furnished him with an introduction to a lady in Rio de Janeiro, the 'Luzitano's' destination. Gauguin was to remember this adventure!

VIROFLAY LANDSCAPE. 1875.
Hernando Uribe Holguin Collection, Bogota.

'I read: Madame Aimée, rue d'Ovidor.

' "You'll see," he told me, "she's a delightful woman, I'm sending you to. She's from Bordeaux, like me."

'The voyage was wonderful, with no storms. As you may imagine, my first thought was to take my little parcel and the letter to the address he had given me. What a pleasure!

' "How sweet of him to have thought of me! And you, let me have a good look at you, dearie. How pretty you are." At that time I was

BUST OF METTE GAUGUIN. 1878.
Courtauld Institute, London.

very small, and although I was seventeen and a half, I looked about fifteen. All the same, I had already fallen into evil ways for the first time before sailing from Le Havre, and my heart was thumping wildly. For me that month was absolutely delicious.'

Gauguin recalls several other incidents from his life as a sailor, but these have little relevance to his later life as a painter. After two voyages to Rio and back, he transferred as second lieutenant to the 'Chili', this time indeed a three-master of over one thousand, two hundred tons, and set off on a journey around the world.

At the beginning of 1868 he was nineteen and had to complete his service. He now held the position of bunker-hand on the corvette 'Jerome-Napoleon', which was in use as Imperial Prince Jerome's yacht. He sailed from the Channel to the Mediterranean, and cruised past the Italian and Greek islands as far as the Black Sea. From bunker-hand he moved up to helmsman, and Gauguin was able to watch scenery that was constantly changing, helping him somehow to endure the discipline of the Imperial Navy. He was almost court-martialled for insolence to a leading-seaman.

Gauguin was surely to remember very little of these travels, for they were made under circumstances that were hardly conducive to poetic contemplation. Added to his childhood impressions of Peru, these five years in the marines must have developed in him a spirit of adventure. Travel for him had become a habit, if not a pleasure, and later he never shared the reluctance of his friends to embark on journeys. These early years at sea left him, if not exactly unstable, certainly ready to leave at any opportunity that he found attractive.

On 19th July 1870, when the Franco-Prussian war broke out, the 'Jerome-Napoleon' had just altered course for Boulogne. Despite the alarming news, she had continued her journey beyond the Arctic Circle and had reached the island of Tromsöe. On 4th September the Empire became the Republic. The 'Jerome-Napoleon' now became the 'Desaix' and distinguished herself by capturing several German vessels. At the beginning of 1871, just as the war was coming to an end, the 'Desaix' reached the Mediterranean, and Gauguin was finally demobilized on 23rd April at Toulon. A new life was to begin.

HIS GUARDIAN'S INFLUENCE

When the military man is demobilized, he returns to his family. Gauguin however no longer had any family. His mother had died in 1867. The house at Saint-Cloud, where his sister had continued to live, had been destroyed with all the family belongings in the bombardment, and his sister had married a Chilean merchant, Juan Uribe.

RUE CARCEL IN THE SNOW. 1882.
Ny Carlsberg Glyptothek, Copenhagen.

There remained only his guardian, Gustave Arosa. Obsessed by the idea of death and anxious for her children's future, Aline Gauguin had altered her will when Paul joined the marines and had appointed this old and generous family friend as their guardian. The following extracts from the will are significant:

'... To my daughter I give my furniture, my linen, lace and cashmere, and to Paul my books, my watch and chain and fob, as well as the signet-ring that belonged to my grandfather ...

'... Further, my express wish is that during her year of mourning, Marie should be placed in a pension at Orleans ... when she has passed the year of mourning in retreat, Monsieur Arosa should find her a position in business, if he thinks this appropriate, or whatever he deems suitable for a woman.

'As for my dear son, he must make his own career, *for he was so unsuccessful in making himself loved by any of my friends,* that he may well find himself entirely abandoned.' (The italics in this passage are our own, for here is evidence of the opinion his mother had formed of the young Gauguin, if not proof of early manifestations of the darker side of his character.)

Gustave Arosa was not only a financier and partner to a stockbroker, he was also an enlightened collector of paintings. A passionate admirer of Delacroix, he had attended the posthumous sale in the artist's studio in 1864, and acquired a number of important works, paintings, drawings and sketches, which had taken their place on his walls alongside his nine Corots, his Daumiers, his seven Courbets and his Jongkinds. He now took Paul Gauguin into his home, where he found himself surrounded by an atmosphere of luxury which he had not known for many years. Arosa shared with Gauguin his taste for painting; and he found him work as a broker's clerk in the offices of a stock-broker named Paul Bertin at 1 rue Laffitte. It was a position that required no specialised knowledge. He simply had to go on his round, collecting and passing on instructions for stock-exchange dealings.

From being a sailor, Gauguin now appeared as a dandy, and after a few differences with his colleagues, kept himself aloof from them.

He worked hard, and whereas before the Peace Treaty he, like the stock-exchange, had been in sorry circumstances, he did well, and was very soon making a good living. Bertin, his employer, had faith in him, and with his permission Gauguin began to speculate on his own account.

On Sundays in the Arosa home at Saint-Cloud Marguerite Arosa, his guardian's daughter, would lend him her brushes and encourage him to paint – in the manner of Corot. Gauguin began to visit the museums and galleries near his office in rue Laffitte. He led a rather retiring bachelor existence. He had his own apartment at 15 rue La Bruyère, and took his meals at Madame Aubé's, a boarding-house. It was here that in 1872 he met two young Danish girls, Marie Heegard and Mette Gad, who was to become his wife. Pola Gauguin, Paul Gauguin's youngest son, today a man of eighty, has recalled the atmosphere and the character of his mother's family in his book, *Paul Gauguin, mon père* (My father, Paul Gauguin).

When the magistrate of the little Danish island of Laeso, Theodor Carl died, at the age of forty, his wife Emilie Lund took her five children and went to live in Copenhagen with her mother, who was a lieutenant-colonel's widow. The old lady was lively and witty, the mother an active and dynamic person, and with only a modest income for their support the girls grew up in a house full of gaiety, where young people of marriageable age were always made welcome in a warm and friendly atmosphere. Mette Sophie Gad, the eldest daughter, conscious of her responsibilities, was the most reserved and the quietest of them. She decided to start work when she was still very young, and took a position as a children's governess with the family of the Minister of State, Estrup, where she educated herself and learned French. It was the knowledge of this language that qualified her to be engaged as travelling companion to Marie Heegaard, a young friend of her own age, the daughter of a wealthy industrialist, who was going on a visit to Paris. The two young girls settled in at the Pension Aubé, and despite their shyness, these two blond Scandinavians must surely have been extremely popular with the young Parisians of 1872.

OUTSKIRTS OF ROUEN. 1884.
Private Collection.

Mette Sophie Gad, a pretty girl, tall and well-built, with an independent nature had already had the experience of an unhappy relationship with a naval officer, when she was attracted to Paul Gauguin, and he to her. However disastrous its consequences may have been for both of them, their marriage was to play an important role in the life of one of the greatest artists of the century.

At this time Gauguin was leading a perfectly calm and well-ordered bachelor existence, and was more interested in his career

NUDE STUDY, OR SUZANNE SEWING. 1880.
Engineer Jens Erik Werenskiold Lysaker Collection, Oslo.

than in any involvements with women (he is not known to have had any). In a photograph taken in 1873 he looks a very shy and hesitant young man. His thick brown, curling hair was cut short and swept back in a dark mass. The mouth is uncertain, and his lower lip has not yet taken on that disdainful curl which was to become progressively more marked in his numerous self-portraits. His nose, which we know was hooked, here appears somewhat strong. The only shadow in the portrait, if such it can be called, is the veiled look in his eyes, a dreamy and nostalgic look under half-closed, rather heavy lids. He was then twenty-five years old, a handsome, dark young man, attractive, full of vitality and ardour.

Mette Sophie Gad is known to us by a terracotta by Gauguin himself, which Bouillot, the sculptor, later carved in marble. A tall blonde with pale eyes, a straight, determined nose, well-defined mouth, an energetic chin and rounded cheeks, she was a personality, sure of herself, resolute, possibly somewhat authoritarian, a woman who knew what mattered to her, and cared little for anything else. For many women, marriage, security and comfort are sufficient aims in life. But it is also more than likely that Mette Sophie was attracted by Paul's charm and by the strange quality that could even then be detected in his eyes. Here was a confrontation of two different races. The cold Northerner was drawn to the saturnine Southerner, in whom there flowed Spanish blood. Conversely, Gauguin was seeking a complementary soul in this Nordic girl.

There is another fact worth noting. Although Paul Gauguin's childhood was one of upheaval, and subsequently he had travelled widely, his character was as yet undeveloped. Until this time he had never had to face up to the full responsibilities of life. He had hardly left the 'Desaix' when the Arosa family filled the role of new parents, who took charge of him, and laid out a path for him to follow without there being any need for him to make any choice or decisions. His marriage was thus the first independent action he was to take; for the first time he undertook something completely on his own initiative, and, moreover, with the full approval of his guardian. He was not aware of what he was doing, and far more serious, he did not yet know what he himself was. Borne along by the routine of his work at the stock-exchange, and sharing the life of the Arosas, he believed himself to be like them. To be married is the normal and logical thing. Possibly he already felt in some confused way that he lacked something, that made him different from his colleagues on the stock-exchange. This something, could it be a wife? I cannot help feeling that Gauguin's marriage was an attempt on his part to become normal and make himself like everyone else. This explanation, like all hypotheses made in retrospect, is only of value in so far as it helps us to understand the subsequent course of events.

Mette Sophie, who was only two years younger than Paul, already had sound experience of life. At the age of twenty-three she had been earning her living for six years in other people's homes, and benefitting from certain advantages and privileges that went with such positions. She possessed the maturity and the strength that were altogether lacking in Paul, if one is to go by his photograph. Like many men who have had no father, and have lived little with their mother, he displayed a need for security and protection. She was to be both a mother and a wife to him. He had need of her, but not in the way usually associated with marriage. When one re-reads all the letters from Gauguin to his wife, one has the feeling that this relationship would have been quite idyllic, had it been between mother and son. But there are things a wife cannot accept. By the time Gauguin had found himself and become aware of his strength it was to be too late. He was by then the father of a family, and this burden was to be a source of self-reproach to him for the whole of his life.

MARRIED LIFE

Gauguin's married life was to last eleven years. It came to an end in 1885 when he left Denmark with his son, Clovis, leaving his wife and his other children behind. But he believed that it was only a temporary separation.

THE SCULPTOR AUBÉ AND HIS SON. 1882.
Musée du Petit Palais, Paris.

In 1873 Mette Sophie returned to Denmark to announce her engagement. She soon came back to France, and the marriage took place on 22nd November 1873 in the town hall of the IXth *arrondissement* in Paris. The couple set up home in a small apartment at 28 Place Saint-Georges, furnished in the style of that period. Gauguin had been promoted in his work; he was now an official assignee on the stock-exchange, and was in a position to be able to afford oriental carpets and precious porcelain. Political events had their repercussions on the stock-exchange, at the time when the constitution of the 3rd Republic was drawn up, but Gauguin's own position merely improved. However, he rarely went out, and took no part in the social life of his colleagues. He remained by the fireside with

28

his young wife, spending a great deal of time reading, and trying his hand at drawing. These modest and somewhat clumsy sketches, displaying nevertheless a developed sense of observation, resemble those touching family photos taken nowadays by amateur photographic enthusiasts.

With the birth of their eldest son, Emile, on 31st August 1874, Paul Gauguin's paternal love was aroused, and to judge from the touching letters he sent to his wife's friends in Denmark, one would certainly believe him to be the most wonderful father!

In 1875 Galichon took over from Bertin as head of the office, but this only served to consolidate Gauguin's position there, and in 1877 he moved to more spacious accommodation in Vaugirard, at 74 rue des Fourneaux, which is today on the corner of the Impasse Frémin and the Cité Falguière. It was a very long way from the stock-exchange ... By now art had already taken a place in his life. Two sculptor friends lived close by—Bouillot and Aubé. But the move was made necessary by the birth in that year of a daughter, called Aline, after her paternal grandmother. They had few worries. Gauguin had begun to invest heavily on the stock-exchange, and was making a lot of money. It was a period of prosperity, such as had been unknown for many years. Gauguin dressed expensively and elegantly, and drove to the stock-exchange in a brougham, which would wait for him until the day's dealings were over.

On 10th May 1879 his third child, Clovis, was born, named after Gauguin's father. In 1880, as a result of continued speculation and much to the amazement and envy of his friends, Gauguin was earning as much as 40,000 gold francs, which in present currency would amount to about £9,000. He allowed this to go to his head a little, and lived on a grand scale, gave money to his wife, who apparently took very little notice of him, immersed as she was in the domesticity of running her home and bringing up her children. Gauguin took good advantage of this prosperity; he moved again, this time to an expensive fine detached house at 8 rue Carcel, still in Vaugirard, which was then no more than a suburban district, and

RUE CARCEL IN THE SNOW. 1883.
Mrs Eva Kiaer Collection, Copenhagen.

FLOWERS IN A BASKET. 1885.
Mrs William Coxe Wright Collection, Philadelphia.

did not become part of the municipality of Paris until later. There
was plenty of room here, a huge studio, and a rather large garden,
which Gauguin painted several times when it lay covered by snow.
Here was a place where he could withdraw.

He also fulfilled another of his dreams—to possess a collection of
paintings, and he invested nearly 15,000 gold francs in one go on
modern paintings and drawings. Was this merely a form of investment, and self-indulgence (in imitation of his guardian, Gustave
Arosa), or was it evidence of a more profound need to surround
himself with the work of artists that pleased him, several of whom

had already become his friends? The collection consisted of works by Pissarro, Guillaumin, Renoir, Monet, Sisley, Degas, Cézanne, Mary Cassatt, Daumier, Jongkind, Lewis-Brown and Manet.

Whereas his wife could not understand how it was possible to spend so much money on works for which she had little feeling, one cannot help admiring Gauguin's unerring taste. This was not necessarily an instance of unaccountable foresight, for the Impressionists were now no longer banned and their exhibitions had ceased to arouse the derision of the multitude. Nevertheless they were far from being accepted by the general public. The Impressionists had only acquired a limited notoriety. Besides, they were still young. In the year 1880 Pissarro was fifty years old, Manet forty-eight, Degas forty-six, Cézanne and Sisley forty-one, Monet forty, Renoir and Guillaumin thirty-nine. This was the year of their fifth group exhibition at 10 rue des Pyramides. Gauguin exhibited paintings for the first time, while as a result of disagreements among the members, Monet refused to take part.

So the industrious assignee of Galichon's stock-brokers' office became a painter, and rather more than an amateur, since he had the honour of contributing to the most dynamic group exhibition of the time, which was to revolutionize all painting and influence artists all over the world. To understand how this came to pass we must go back over several years and trace several facts, whose significance could not be appreciated at the time.

'SCHUFF' – A COLLEAGUE UNLIKE THE OTHERS

In 1905 Madame Paul Gauguin, widow of the artist, told Jean de Rotonchamp, who wrote one of the best monographs of Gauguin ever to appear: 'No one gave Paul the idea of painting. He painted because he could not do otherwise, and when we got married I had no idea that he had any talent for the arts. Once we were married, he painted every Sunday. Sometimes he would go to Colarossi's studio, but he never thought of a teacher ...' It seems that this inescapable vocation, which was to take him so far afield and bring him glory and solitude, only became apparent at a comparatively late stage in his life, and after numerous circumstances had coincided.

In the house at Saint-Cloud, his guardian's daughter, Marguerite, had already started him off by showing him how to use the brushes, and Gauguin had placed his first colour strokes with a delicate and sensitive touch. But there was doubtless more coquetry than vocation in this early 'duet painting'.

Of greater significance by far was his meeting and subsequent friendship with Claude-Emile Schuffenecker, a friendship which was fostered by their constant contact at work in the office of the stock-broker Bertin. Schuffenecker had been orphaned at an early age, and spent his life as a humble employee and then as a civil servant in the Treasury, before securing his present position with Bertin. A small, round, jovial man, he did not work very zealously, nor did he speculate, but he dreamed of becoming a great painter. As soon as he left the office, he went to work in the studios of the masters of the period, Paul Baudry and Carolus-Durand. He was a modest person, two years younger than Paul Gauguin, whom he admired. For his part, Gauguin had at last found someone with whom he could talk about painting. They went together to the Louvre. Finally 'Schuff', as he was called for short, took Gauguin along to Montparnasse, to the Colarossi school in the rue de la Grande Chaumière. On Sundays, they would go out to the suburbs to do 'subject' paintings. Thus, before his marriage, Paul Gauguin was already spending some of his free time in painting. It is worth mentioning that at this time there were a number of art dealers in the rue Laffitte, where his office was, so that he had ample opportunity to study Impressionist works on his way to and from work.

When Gauguin married, Mette Sophie made Schuffenecker welcome, for she found him pleasant and harmless, whereas by encouraging Gauguin to paint he in fact constituted the gravest threat to the happiness of her married life.

When Mette became pregnant Gauguin, who felt obliged to remain with her and keep her company, made numerous pencil drawings of her and when their son was born, he drew her with the baby. Mette

LIBRARY
SOUTHERN UNION STATE JUNIOR COLLEGE

33

DAHLIAS. 1885.
Arthur Sachs Collection.

did not take painting seriously. Besides, at this time Gauguin merely
regarded his painting as a psycho-therapeutic activity, whereby he
sought to escape from his sombre thoughts, or as a form of relaxation
from his professional preoccupations. Nevertheless in the discussions
at the Colarossi studio, he would be extremely rigid in his judgments and sometimes quite violent in his assertions. Painting was
certainly no game for him, for in 1876 he submitted a canvas entitled
Viroflay Landscape (page 18) to the Salon, and much to his sur-

FLOWERS AND A FAN. 1885.
Winthrop Collection, New York.

prise it was accepted by the jury. A critic even remarked upon his entry. It is a work, dominated by the play of light and shade and recalling the Barbizon school. Compared with his first more docile landscapes in the style of Corot, this is already a definite step towards Impressionism.

As a result of this encouragement, Gauguin was to spend more and more of his time painting, sometimes working at night in his studio, and closely following the activities of the artists of the time. The same year the second Impressionist exhibition was held at Durand-Ruel. He sometimes went there to look at the new canvases. One of the group was Camille Pissarro, several of whose paintings Arosa possessed.

CAMILLE PISSARRO'S REVOLUTIONARY IDEAS

The Pissarros in Arosa's collection gave Gauguin a conversational opening when he met the painter. We are familiar with Pissarro's appearance from a self-portrait dated that same year; he was a mature man, with a serious air. Luck was never on his side. He was almost bald, with a long beard that was losing its colour, and looked older than his forty-six years. He held opinions which he regarded as socialist, and which bordered on anarchy. Could this be the reason why he was selling so little, at a time when his friends were beginning to live on their painting? He often let a canvas go for 100 francs. As a Jew he felt persecuted, and this made him preach all the more violently in favour of the new art, Impressionism. Gauguin was swept along by his eloquence. He saw the works of the 'Manet group' in a new light, and was suddenly given a fresh understanding of Monet, Renoir, Degas, Sisley, Cézanne and Berthe Morisot. He was won over to the use of the 'bright palette'. Painting with only three primary colours, blue, red and yellow: here was the secret of a new way of seeing.

Pissarro was born at Saint-Thomas des Antilles, the Danish colony, and Mette welcomed him warmly like a fellow-countryman. Moreover, although he had not attained commercial success, Pissarro

36

MANDOLIN AND FLOWERS. 1885.
Louvre, Paris.

was nevertheless a personality much spoken of and his visits flattered her vanity.

Pissarro was a revolutionary and remained one the whole of his life. He criticized Gauguin for having sent an entry to the Salon, and took him to Place Pigalle, to the Nouvelle Athènes, where the 'Cénacle' composed of painters, poets and men of letters used to meet in a back room. Gauguin was no longer an amateur on his own, he was now part of an organized group, fighting to assert its own concepts. Here, as in the stock-exchange, Gauguin remained in the background, but this was a matter of pride. He kept apart from the others, and made friends only with Guillaumin, who in turn met Mette and came to the house quite often.

Thanks to Pissarro, Gauguin was included in the fourth group exhibition of the Impressionists in 1879, at the Avenue de l'Opéra, contributing a small statuette which he had modelled in clay at the home of his neighbour, the sculptor Bouillot in the rue des Fourneaux. Gauguin appeared as an amateur, his name was not in the catalogue and the Impressionists, uncompromising in the stiff battle they were engaged in, had very mixed feelings about the intrusion of this well-dressed financier.

At the fifth Impressionist exhibition in 1880, held at the rue des Pyramides, Gauguin had an ample showing of seven canvases. Monet voluntarily abstained, decrying the admission of 'any old dauber'. Did this refer to Gauguin? In any case official criticism barely made any distinction between the exhibitors, and for Albert Wolff of the *Figaro* it was no more than an 'agglomeration of nonentities'!

'On leaving the Mirlitons, I went to have a look round the exhibition of artists who call themselves independent or Impressionist. Their small annual showing opened on 1st April on a mezzanine floor in the rue des Pyramides. I had been in no hurry to go and see these things, a few sketches alongside works by misguided individuals who take rough pebbles for precious gems. I exclude Monsieur Degas and Madame Berthe Morisot. But all the rest are not worth looking at, and even less worth discussing. This is mere pretentious emptiness ... Why does a man like Monsieur Degas waste his time amidst such an agglomeration of nonentities? Why does he not do what Manet has long since done, and leave the Impressionists? He was not one to go forever trailing this detestable school behind him . . .'

There is no doubt that Gauguin's painting *La Promenade,* which was shown in this exhibition and dated the same year, is still an awkward, unskilful work. It is not that the figures are barely drawn in–it was a deliberate mannerism of the Impressionists to present them as silhouettes–but the composition is static, there are large areas that have scarcely been modulated, and the problems of space and perspective have not been resolved; the painting leads away to the left and has not been enclosed; it is not firmly fixed within the framework of the canvas. This was a problem that had already been overcome by the Impressionist painters, notably by Pissarro, Degas and Morisot who contributed to the same exhibition. Humiliated by his first experience of the battle for a new art form, Gauguin felt himself inseparably bound up with the Impressionists, but he also realized that it was essential for him to work more, for sensitive as he was, he could not avoid being aware of the difference between his entries and those that hung beside them.

For his time Gauguin was not yet a modern painter. The evidence of this is that he was more successful with classical subjects, like the nude he exhibited the following year with the same group, the sixth of its kind, held at the Boulevard des Capucines. It is strange that this *Nude* (page 25), which was in no way Impressionist, was accepted for such an exhibition. Be that as it may, it attracted the detailed attention of the writer Joris-Karl Huysmans, who wrote:

'Last year Monsieur Gauguin exhibited a series of landscapes which were still a hesitant watering-down of Pissarro. This year Monsieur Gauguin is represented by a canvas that is really his own, a work displaying the indisputable temperament of a modern painter. It is entitled: *Nude Study, or Suzanne sewing.* In the foreground a woman seen in profile is seated on a divan, mending her chemise, a purplish covering stretches away behind her as far as the background, which is cut short by the bottom edge of an Algerian curtain . . .

39

DIEPPE HARBOUR. 1885 (?)
City Art Gallery, Manchester.

'I do not hesitate to state that among all the contemporary artists who have tackled the nude, there is none that has as yet achieved such vehement reality ... The flesh is rudely alive; this is not the smooth, even skin, without spots or bumps or pores, the skin dipped in a vat of pink and then gone over with a warm iron, that all the other artists produce; here is skin beneath which the blood flows and nerves twitch; and finally what truth there is in all the parts of the body, in the large belly that spills over the thighs, in those folds beneath the sagging chin, ringed with dark patches, in the angular knee joints, and in the prominence of the wrist! ...

'Monsieur Gauguin is the first artist in years to have attempted to represent the woman of today ... He has roundly succeeded and has produced a bold and authentic painting.'

For Gauguin this was a virtual recognition of his aims. But J.-K. Huysmans had quite definitely separated him from his Impressionist colleagues whose insistence on atmosphere and shimmering colours were foreign to him. What pleased the critic in this canvas by Gauguin was something unique to the artist, the emphasis on realism. Huysmans was after all a naturalist writer himself, and had not Zola published *L'Assommoir* in 1877 and *Nana* that same year?

PAINTING OUSTS THE STOCK-EXCHANGE

Painting now took an ever larger place in Gauguin's life. He divided his time between painting and sculpture, producing a number of oriental and primitive inspired wooden sculptures. He discovered the Japanese prints that the Goncourt brothers were to make so fashionable, and met more and more artists, including Puvis de Chavannes, who was exhibiting his *Poor Fisherman* at the Salon. Gauguin was sensitive to this condensed form of symbolism which permitted painting to express lofty and vague philosophical and moral ideas.

As in the previous year, he spent his summer holiday with his friend Pissarro, near Pontoise. Cézanne was also working there. 'He's very holy for an artist,' he was to say of Cézanne, 'he's forever playing the organ.' His admiration showed itself when he bought one of Cézanne's paintings for his collection.

Meanwhile prices on the stock-exchange continued to rise. *Union Générale* and the *Banque Catholique* stocks had doubled in price and then increased tenfold. Gauguin envied those of his friends who were able to devote all their time and all their activity to painting. His turn was to come. But was this the ruthless, irresponsible decision all his biographers assume it to have been, or did the financial crash that came in the following year influence him to take this step?

The 1882 Impressionist exhibition took place amidst violent dissension between the members of the group. This time Gauguin, who was barely concerned in the quarrel, took part with astonishing firmness. He wrote to Pissarro:

'If I am to examine your position objectively, I must admit right away that in the ten years since you have taken on these exhibitions, the number of Impressionists has risen, their talent has increased, and their influence too. But on the other hand, as far as Degas is concerned, and it is his doing alone, the trend is going persistently downhill: each year another Impressionist leaves us and makes way for nonentities and schoolboys. Another year or two and you will be all alone among the worst kind of cheap poseurs. All your efforts will be brought to nothing, and Durand-Ruel will be ruined into the bargain.'

STILL LIFE IN AN INTERIOR. 1885.
Private Collection, U.S.A.

THE BEACH AT DIEPPE. 1885.
Ny Carlsberg Glyptothek, Copenhagen.

'With the best will in the world, I cannot see my way to continuing to act the clown for Monsieur Raffaëlli and company. Therefore I must ask you to accept my resignation. From today I shall stay on my own ... I believe that Guillaumin intends to do the same, but I do not wish to influence his decision in any way.'

The situation had undergone a curious reversal. The first Impressionists had always protested against the intrusion of newcomers into the group, particularly when their talent or their qualifications as

Impressionists were debatable. Thus it was that in introducing Gauguin, Pissarro had caused Monet to leave. And now Gauguin was protesting in his turn against the youngsters being brought in by Degas, a man whom he admired, for he was included in his collection. To give some idea of the passionate intensity with which these discussions were conducted, let us quote the following extract of a letter from Claude Monet to the dealer, Durand-Ruel:

'To exhibit alongside Pissarro, Gauguin and Guillaumin, would be like exhibiting alongside social nobodies. The public dislike anything that savours of politics, and I at my age do not wish to be revolutionary ... To remain together with Pissarro, the Jew, means being revolutionary.' Claude Monet should not be too severely judged for his 'exit' which was prompted by a passing fit of temper. It was he himself that said of official medals: 'It is not enough to refuse them, it is more important not to have earned them.'

The exhibition nevertheless took place, for threatened by the *Union Générale* slump, Durand-Ruel now threw all his influence into the balance, and the Impressionists certainly owed him a great deal. Gauguin entered twelve works, which were severely criticized by Monet, Renoir, and even by J.-K. Huysmans.

Artistic life was not the only scene of storms. The stock-exchange was witnessing dramatic hours. Since 11th January prices had been slumping. Several securities disappeared as a result of bankruptcies, spelling ruin for many speculators as well as for small investors. Gauguin was not only earning less but had lost huge sums. He became disinterested and paid little attention to business, taken up as he was with the current aesthetic quarrels and with his fervent desire to make his style develop out of its present deadlock. His colours darkened, and he could not succeed in giving his paintings the composition and the rhythm needed to achieve a powerful impact, to express all that he felt and was trying to express. In this frame of mind, it was but a short step to regarding the time he spent at the stock-exchange as a threat to his future as a painter. It would not have taken much to convince him that he was wasting his time at Galichon's—he was earning so little in comparison with previous years.

FOUR BRETON WOMEN DANCING. 1886.
Bayerische Staatsgemäldesammlungen, Munich.

A number of biographers, giving free reign to their imagination, and seeking to show that Gauguin was destined to his inevitable vocation, have minimised the repercussions of the crash on the stock-exchange in 1882. According to them, Gauguin gave up a profitable position in order to paint; he preferred art and poverty to the gilded cage he inhabited in the office of his employer. This was not exactly the case. One is tempted to ask whether, amidst the financial unrest, Galichon was not happy to accept Gauguin's resignation in order to cut his expenses. One might even go so far as to wonder whether in fact it was Gauguin who left the stock-exchange, or the stock-exchange that dismissed him ... This might certainly apply, did we not know that Gauguin wished with all his heart to have the maximum amount of time to devote to painting. But the decision he took in January 1883 no longer has the same significance. He was not a financier abandoning wealth, but a man who was swayed by events and who seized the opportunity to do something he knew to be risky, despite all his own attempts to reassure himself.

His friends had warned him. Schuffenecker, ever prudent, had left the bank in good time, and used a small inheritance to start a modest business dealing in rolled gold, which brought in enough to provide for him and his family (he had meanwhile married a pretty, slightly vulgar orphan), while leaving him more free time to paint. He did not take the crisis seriously, and whereas other more famous artists found it difficult to live by their painting, Gauguin could count on selling enough to live on. It was Pissarro, pursued by misfortune all his life, and whose exhibition had been seen by very few people, (Sisley's had been even more catastrophic) who expressed his most profound belief to Gauguin: 'If one is compelled to paint in order to live, one risks sacrificing one's personality to public taste.' He was somewhat shocked by Gauguin's obvious desire to 'arrive':

'He [Gauguin] is terribly commercially minded. I dare not tell him how wrong this is, and how little it helps him. His requirements are very great, and it is true his family is accustomed to luxurious living, but this will do him great harm. Not that I think one should not attempt to sell, but I think it a waste of time to think of that alone; you lose sight of your art, you over-estimate your value.'

Gauguin rejected this wise counsel, which incidentally hardly ever helped Pissarro himself. He needed to give himself confidence, and during the whole of his life he never lost his incorrigible optimism, that bordered on unreason.

ROUEN, FIRST STAGE OF EXILE

Gauguin could not have saved much money. The difficulties soon began. His wife was unwilling to accept a cut in her budget. As on

46

several occasions at this period of his life, Gauguin now followed the example of Pissarro, who had gone to live in Rouen, this being much cheaper than living in Paris. But Mette was pregnant and he had to wait until 6th December when their fifth child was born; his name was Paul-Rollon, known as Pola.

Meanwhile he painted the snow-covered garden of the house in the rue Carcel for the last time (page 30), putting great nostalgia and melancholy into it. He also painted the first of his many self-portraits. Gauguin was now as we know him, with those features that were to become increasingly pronounced – the low forehead, slightly protruding eyes, sidelong glance, the bitter slant of the mouth emphasized by the drooping moustache. He painted himself standing in front of his easel, palette and brush in hand, showing that he really was an artist. But his comfortable clothes and short hair are still those of an easy-going bank official, given to dreaming of being someone else.

Gauguin travelled to Rouen for the first time, where he saw Pissarro, and, judging by Pissarro's correspondence, the meeting was probably not very reassuring. But Gauguin was confident of the future, even though he had not yet found a picture-dealer. He rented a house in Rouen, 5 Impasse Malerne, and returned to Paris to arrange the move. In January 1884, the whole family arrived in Rouen and settled in with the five children and the maid. Doubtless Mette did not agree to give up her house and all the prestige attached to it without strongly defending her point of view and what she considered to be her children's interest. After a stormy argument she accepted, for there still remained the hope of regaining a comfortable and dignified life in Rouen. Once there, however, one disappointment followed another, and she lost all faith in her husband. The situation became intolerable for her.

It is surprising that Gauguin found the time and especially the energy and the courage to paint a few harbour scenes during this short stay. There was no doubt that this was going to be a permanent conflict. The bitterness that had built up in his wife over the last months, her constant complaints and recriminations threw a new light on their eleven years of uneventful married life together. Mette

BRETON LANDSCAPE. 1888 (?)
National Gallery, Washington.

had married a business man whose fortunes had soared unexpectedly.
Had he painted just for relaxation, she would have regarded this as
perfectly normal. But that the father of a large family should throw
up his position without warning in order to devote himself to painting, when his talent was far from being recognized, and when he had
no prospect of selling his work, this appeared insane to her. And it
is quite easy to see her point of view. She regarded her husband as
irresponsible, nourishing ill-founded illusions. She did not see this as
a change in him, for her it was betrayal. The woman who had openly
admitted being 'first and foremost a mother' was afraid. Unless

Gauguin already had a clear awareness, a sort of premonition of his own genius at this time, it is difficult to understand why he stubbornly refused to do anything to reassure her. Probably he tried to do this before leaving Paris – he may well have taken steps to join the bank again, only to be politely turned down. This would support the theory that his heroic decision to abandon all for the sake of his painting was not quite so spontaneous, though historic for all that. There was such a slump in the business world, that once out of it, it was impossible even for a man like Gauguin to get back in.

Reacting in the typically feminine way, Mette turned to her mother. She went on her first visit back to Copenhagen with her two youngest

VISION AFTER THE SERMON. 1888.
National Gallery of Scotland, Edinburgh.

children, leaving Gauguin alone with the three others and the maid, and time to straighten things out. In Denmark she renewed her family ties, and considered the possibility of fending for herself, by giving French lessons and doing translations. Paul might possibly even find work worthy of him, she hoped. In October she returned to Rouen. Once again there were quarrels and endlessly recurring scenes, only this time they were more serious. Mette was not leaving him temporarily, she was moving out and taking everything with her, furniture, linen and crockery. Gauguin felt abandoned; he could not bear it. In desperation he managed to find money for the journey by taking on the agency for Dillies & Co. of Roubaix, manufacturers of waterproof, imperishable fabrics. Proud of this new position, and once again filled with optimism, he followed Mette to Copenhagen.

DISILLUSIONMENT IN COPENHAGEN

The meeting with the family was no honeymoon, and the Gauguins quickly found an apartment in the new district of Gammel Kongevej. There was seldom any money coming in, and despite the French lessons she was giving, Mette found herself in an unfavourable situation, compared with her sisters. Her inferior position made her suffer, and she retaliated with bad temper. Following up introductions given to him by his Danish brothers-in-law, Gauguin tried unsuccessfully to interest naval and railway buyers in his imperishable fabrics. No one ever refused him outright, and the polite evasions undermined his morale. Meanwhile Messrs Dillies & Co. were losing patience.

Small wonder that he sought refuge in painting! Every free moment was spent painting and reflecting on art. His paintings were to stay with his wife in Copenhagen. One of the best known is a landscape, *The Queen's Mill in Oestervold Park*. His palette had brightened, but was still dark compared with the Impressionists. His thick, even, close-set brush strokes reflect a determined, serious character. On the whole there was no marked development in his style, but it was more the time spent in reflection and in exploration of technical possibilities which made the winter of 1884–85 significant in his career.

He confided in his old friend Schuffenecker who at that time was struggling to set up a new Salon in Paris which was to be known as the 'Independents'. Gauguin wrote to him on 14th January 1885:

'Here art torments me more than ever, and neither my money worries nor my attempts at business can distract me from it. You say that I would do well to join your Society of Independents; shall I tell you what will happen? There are a hundred of you, tomorrow there will be two hundred. Two-thirds of them are commercially-minded intriguers; in no time at all people like Gervex and others will take over, and then what will happen to us, the dreamers, the misunderstood? This year you had a 'favourable press', next year they (there are Raffaëllis everywhere) will be stirring up the mud to spatter you with, in order to look respectable themselves.

'Work "freely and furiously" and you will make progress, and sooner or later your talent will be recognized, if you have any. But above all, do not labour over a painting; a strong sentiment can be expressed immediately, think about it and look for the simplest way.

'As far as business is concerned, I am still right at the beginning, I shall not see any results for another six months. Meanwhile, I haven't a penny, and am fed up to the teeth, which is why I comfort myself in dreaming.'

Since there appeared to be hardly any market for imperishable fabrics and he had to live somehow, Gauguin now tried to sell his paintings, and agreed to exhibit in a private show at the Society of Friends of Art. This was yet another cruel source of disappointment, for it touched what lay closest to Gauguin, his pride as an artist, and his confidence in his own talent. Hardly anyone went to the show, and there was not a single line in the press. Yet when exhibitions of Gauguin's work were held in Copenhagen in 1891 and 1893 the critics were to remember this first exhibition and were to refer to it in their articles. But in 1885 the Danish patrons of the arts were not yet sufficiently enlightened to accept Impressionism. He referred to this affront in a letter to Schuffenecker, dated 25th May 1885:

'I have held an exhibition of my works here, and one day I shall tell you how after five days they closed it and how the violently

BRETON BOYS BATHING. 1888.
Hamburg Museum.

enthusiastic newspaper articles were suppressed. All the basest intrigues! All the old academic clan were shaking at the possible outcome, which is very flattering for an artist, but has a disastrous effect.'

He could not believe such stupidity existed, and as he could not imagine that his painting was bad, he immediately suspected a conspiracy and intrigues; perhaps for the first time, he felt persecuted, for this was the obsession that was to remain with him for the rest of his life, alternating with equally unjustified moods of optimistic vanity:

'I have been the victim of a few Protestant bigots here, they know I am an unbeliever and would like to see my downfall. The Jesuits are saints compared with religious Protestantism, and so Countess de Motke, who was paying for my son Emile's schooling has withdrawn her support, on religious grounds, you understand. And there is nothing I can do. A lot of the French lessons have stopped for the same reason, etc . . . it is all getting a bit much for me, and I long to throw up everything and come to Paris, where I could work and earn just enough to keep me going, as assistant sculptor for Bouillot, and I would be free. Duty! Just let someone else try it, I've done all I possibly could, and I yield before the sheer impossibility of carrying on this way. Once again thanks for all the interest you've taken in us, there are not that many people who still value you when you're down on your luck!'

All these incidents made his relationship with his wife deteriorate even further, and the atmosphere in his home grew continually worse. Their money worries became more and more pressing, and they had to move once again to a smaller apartment at 51 Norregade. But Gauguin was far too proud to complain. He only touches upon this right at the end of the letter to 'Schuff':

'My wife tells me to send her kindest regards to yours. She is not a pleasant person at the moment. Poverty has completely embittered her, and it is especially her vanity that suffers (in this country where everyone knows one another), and I put up with all the complaints. Of course, if it weren't for my painting, I would still be a successful stock-broker, etc . . .'

THE WHITE TABLECLOTH. 1886.
Michael Astor Collection, London.

Such bitterness and so many insults were heaped upon Gauguin that he decided to return to Paris by train, with his favourite son, Clovis. R. Cogniat came upon the itinerary for this journey on the back of a sketch book. Seventeen years later, as he wrote his memoirs, he recalled all the hatred he had felt for the country that had given him such a cool welcome. There was nothing, not the way of life, nor the museums, nor its artists, nor its women that found favour in his eyes, and he brought up all the old grudges he bore it.

PORTRAIT OF PHILIBERT FAVRE. 1885.
Private Collection, Paris.

'I hate Denmark bitterly. Its climate, and its inhabitants. Oh, that there is some good in Denmark is undeniable.

'Thus whereas for the past twenty-five years Norway and Sweden have been flocking to the exhibitions of painting in France in order to plagiarize all that appeals to them, however bad, Denmark, humiliated by her failure at the Universal Exhibition of 1878, has begun to reflect and look inwards. The outcome of this has been a Danish art, that is highly individual and which must be considered quite seriously, and I am pleased in this instance to be able to praise it. To examine French art, and even the art of all the other countries is good, but only in order to be in a better position to examine oneself.'

'. . . I admit that the system of betrothal in Denmark is a good thing in the sense that it is not binding (people change fiancés like we change a vest), and then it has all the outward appearances of love, liberty and being moral. You are engaged, well then, go for walks together, even on holiday. The cloak of betrothal is there to cover all. You play at everything, except the one thing, the advantage of which is that it teaches the two partners not to forget themselves and do anything foolish. Very practical people, the Danes . . . See for yourself, but don't get involved. You might regret it, and always remember that the Danish girl is the most practical of all women . . . Moreover, never forget that it is a small country—and you must be prudent. Even for the small children, whom you are only just teaching to say "Papa", you need cash, otherwise, my poor father, nothing doing. I have known what it's like.

'I hate the Danes.'

THE FABLE OF THE DOG AND THE WOLF

The year 1885 was an important date in the life of Gauguin and in the history of art. It is worth while investigating Gauguin's position at this decisive moment in his destiny.

In 1884 the Salon des Indépendants had been founded. Odilon Redon published some albums of lithographs whose new spirit marked a turning point in aesthetics. Renoir underwent a crisis, which was decisive for his development. Cézanne now saw the composition of all forms in the simple geometric terms of the sphere, cube and pyramid, the principle that led to Cubism. Toulouse-Lautrec arrived in Montmartre and discovered the world of the music-halls and brothels, which was to provide him with his favourite subjects. Seurat and Signac began to apply their division of colour tones and painted their first pointillist works. Van Gogh finally made up his mind to leave his own country and come to Paris.

56

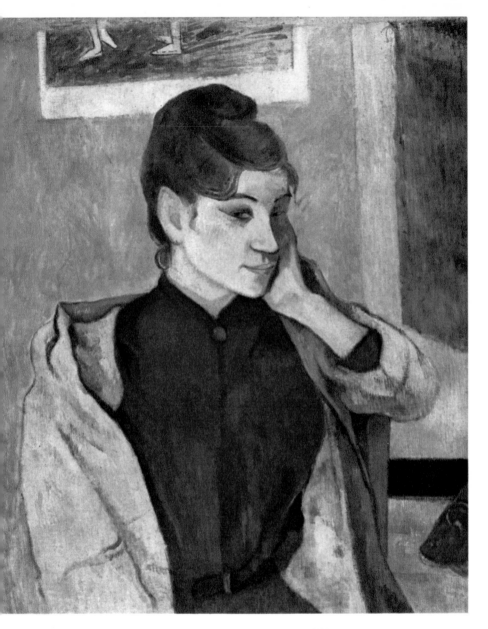

PORTRAIT OF MADELEINE BERNARD. 1888.
Musée de Grenoble.

Modern art was being born. In the expression of pure feeling, the Impressionists had reached the ultimate conclusions of reality. Artists were to react against an art that consisted of nothing more than a reproduction of reality, and reject the external features of nature in their insistence on expressing themselves. Even the concept of the beautiful was changing. This was the birth of modern art. Its aim was no longer to reproduce an ideal form of beauty, but to serve as a means of communication between men.

Gauguin had chosen freedom, his own personal freedom. He had abandoned his wife and children in order to devote himself completely to painting. This is the official version of his story. The genius made manifest in his works was to justify the apparent cowardice of his behaviour. Even the most moral minded of art-lovers, who firmly supported the principles of bourgeois society, were to accept this attitude, since it was Gauguin that was concerned. Such is the stature of the artist when he finally comes to be recognized that everything can be forgiven. However, this is not a reliable interpretation of the facts. A close examination of the correspondence between Gauguin and his wife reveals her family's attitude as a determined effort to make his life intolerable, accusing him of allowing himself to be kept. Thus they were responsible for putting the idea of flight in his head.

This is the theory supported by René Huyghe, Keeper of the Department of Paintings and Drawings in the Louvre at the time of the Gauguin Centenary Exhibition which was held during the summer of 1949. In a study included in the catalogue he quotes numerous extracts from letters that lend weight to this point of view: 'As soon as my affairs improve, I firmly intend to take back the other children. You know I have the right to do so.' (25th April 1886) '. . . Now that your sister has succeeded in driving me away . . .' (9th August 1885) '. . . I am quite sure it was your sister's doing. Admittedly I have suffered a harsh blow, but I can stand up to it.' (19th September 1885), etc.

An objective analysis of the facts confirms that his in-laws helped Gauguin to make his decision. Had things been on a cordial and amicable footing when he left, there would have been no reason for him to take his son Clovis with him, who would surely have been better off at his mother's side. He had burdened himself with a six-year-old child in order to assert his paternal rights, holding the child as a hostage, as it were. This is the more likely explanation, especially since Gauguin no longer travelled with a well-lined wallet, ensuring every comfort, nor with a nurse to look after the child. His present material situation was most precarious, since he had very little money, and did not know where or how he would live, or eat. Such was his irresponsibility in dragging a child along with him that this can only be justified, or at least explained, as an act of protest.

These reflections are not an attempt either on the part of René Huyghe or myself to detract in any way from the poetic nature of Gauguin's life, but are a quest for the historical truth, for a better understanding of the man, and a more accurate interpretation of his behaviour. Too many legends attach themselves to famous men, and at a distance of sixty years it is difficult to establish the true motives for certain actions. Just as the crash on the stock-exchange coincided with his resignation, similarly the hostile attitude of the Gad family caused him to leave Copenhagen.

To devote himself entirely to his art ... This was the hope with which Gauguin returned to Paris. But, ironically, the most bitter disappointment lay in store for him. He was not even given the humble work that he had been led to count on, and which would have brought in enough for him and his son to live on. Every moment of his time and all his endeavours were now devoted to the hard task of surviving at a time when France found herself in economic straits. He had been promised a job as sculptor's assistant to Bouillot, who was expecting a commission. It is the assistant's task to rough-hew the block of stone or marble, and sometimes to finish off the work. In order to be close at hand, Gauguin moved into the Impasse Frémin, near his former home in the rue des Foureaux, but meanwhile the delay dragged on, and when Bouillot secured the commission his client compelled him to use a different assistant.

Meanwhile he was continually being pursued by Dillies & Co., for he had not returned the advances they had made him. This was

PORTRAIT OF ROULIN'S SON. 1888.
Private Collection, Basle.

MARTINIQUE LANDSCAPE. 1887.
Private Collection, Paris.

yet another worry. Gauguin had left Copenhagen with virtually no clothing and no linen. Mette was supposed to send him these, but the cases were slow in arriving. The letters he wrote his wife give some insight into what this first year of poverty must have meant for a man accustomed to want for nothing.

9th August: 'I still have not had my case ... Winter will soon be here, and I shall have nothing in which to work ...'

19th August: 'I still have no news of the case, so you might go and complain to them in Copenhagen, as it was quite correctly addressed ... Everything is still the same, I have no linen, one of the dealer's advertised my pictures, and I shall probably lose sales ...'

Beginning of October: 'You don't intend to give your brothers my fur coat, do you? I should very much have liked you to send it to me ... At the moment I only have my summer trousers, which are getting very shabby, and anyway they are beginning to look ridiculous in this cold weather...'

Gauguin rented a small apartment near the Gare du Nord at 10 rue Cail. On 13th October he wrote: 'Clovis goes to school close by, and the concierge looks after him... It would be as well if you could send him a jersey for he is not properly dressed.'

20th October: 'At present Clovis sleeps on a small bed I have hired and I use a mattress and my travelling rug... Don't worry about Clovis... Food is no problem... An egg and a little rice make a very good meal for him, particularly when there is an apple to follow.'

End of November: 'It is bitterly cold at the moment, and I could well do with a mattress and some blankets... For the last month I have been sleeping on a plank, wrapped in my travelling rug.'

THE DEPTHS OF POVERTY

All through the winter Gauguin's material position grew steadily worse. He never gave up the struggle, looking for work, no matter how menial, and attempted to sell even very cheaply those of his paintings his wife had sent him. He faced up to the harsh blows dealt him by fate with a stubbornness that never deserted him. As a man who at times yielded easily to the false calls of destiny, when driven to extremes he was nevertheless able to call upon unsuspected reserves of energy. He even went as far as comforting his wife when she complained of her loneliness and other trivial problems.

'You are in *your own* very comfortably furnished house, doing a laborious job, but one which you like, you see people, and since you like the company of Danish people, you ought to find satisfaction sometimes... Whereas I have been driven from my home, I live anywhere, between four walls, with a bed, a table, no heating, and seeing no one. Clovis behaves like a hero, when we sit down together at our table in the evening, to our piece of bread and meat. He forgets how greedy he used to be, he keeps quiet, and asks for nothing, not even to play, and goes straight to bed.'

There is a cry of revolt that breaks through this dutiful and conventional tone, protesting against the misfortune that was pursuing him: 'Necessity makes its own laws, and sometimes it forces men out of the positions imposed upon them by society. When the boy fell ill with smallpox, I had twenty centimes in my pocket and we had been eating dry bread on credit for three days... I was panic-striken. I worked as a bill-sticker at five francs a day; meanwhile Clovis was in bed with fever, and in the evening I would go to him and look after him.'

Humiliation made Gauguin suffer deeply. But he put on a show of indifference – he wanted to humiliate Mette by the account of his own downfall. His rancour against her is imaginable, and he wished to torture her by making her suffer anguish over the health of her son. Gauguin was indeed a strange combination of devotion and moral faithfulness on the one hand, and obstinacy and passion that could altogether get the better of him on the other. His sadness in these letters at the tearless resignation with which the little boy accepted his shared life with his father is very moving. This slightly melodramatic, but sincere tone runs all the way through Gauguin's correspondence, but in his memoirs, *Avant et Après*, written a short time before his death, he gave vent to such malice and shameless fabrication that his biographers are continually obliged to emphasize the liberties he took with the truth.

GAUGUIN AS A POLITICAL AGENT?

There remains one mysterious episode in the course of Gauguin's otherwise all too familiar life. What were the reasons for his secret visit to London in September 1885? He had no money, so his journey must have been financed. He embarked at Dieppe, and it was here that he wrote to his wife: 'I am going on a journey; I am spending two or three days here in Dieppe, before going on to London where I shall stay for three weeks, *you know where.* As you must know from the Copenhagen newspapers the Spanish business is getting more involved, which is all to the good as far as

MARTINIQUAN EVE. 1887.
Ny Carlsberg Glyptothek, Copenhagen.

the little development we are aiming for is concerned. Now it is only a matter of time, and I have not failed to go and renew a certain friendship. For the future then it is *virtually a certainty*.'

The mystery remains complete, and up to the present no facts have emerged that would give any clue as to the connections Gauguin might have had with people in exile. However, if one is to believe Schuffenecker, according to his *Notes on Gauguin,* in 1883 Gauguin is supposed to have smuggled Ruiz Zorilla, the leader of the republican party and former president of the council, over the Spanish border after the failure of the Estramadura revolt and the rising of the Badajoz garrison. This kind of escapade, the flight concealed in a haycart, must have fired Gauguin's romantic imagination. Perhaps Pissarro had put him in touch with the Spanish revolutionaries, but this cannot be proved. Similarly any link between

TURKEYS. 1888.
William Goetz Collection, Los Angeles

these two episodes is mere conjecture, and can only be justified in so far as it sheds light on Gauguin's adventurous character.

This journey gave the painter a few days' relaxation at Dieppe, where a whole colony of artists was holidaying—Degas, Jacques-Emile Blanche, Whistler, Sickert, Helleu. It was just as much his own inclination as reasons of economy that now led him to dress in the unconventional manner he was to maintain all his life. No doubt anxious to conceal his hardship, he posed as the outcast artist, and was looked upon as an eccentric, indeed as a 'megalomaniac'.

But Gauguin cared nothing for this, and certainly not at the way he aroused smiles wherever he went. He was able to paint a few bold canvases in his own style of Impressionism—harbour scenes (page 40) or peasant women on the sea-shore (page 43). These show a greater confidence and freedom than in the past, and in one still life there is the as yet still hesitant dark outline, which he developed the following year at Pont-Aven, and which was to become one of the characteristics of the 'cloisonnist' style.

Back in Paris during these months of famine, friends were few and far between. Occasionally Gauguin dined at the homes of Jobbé-Duval and of Schuffenecker, who was now exulting in his appointment as drawing master at the Lycée Michelet at Vanves in the outskirts of Paris, a position he had coveted for a number of years. Both he and Gauguin took part in the eighth and last Impressionist exhibition. Too many disagreements had disrupted the group, and most of the original members had left to be replaced by newcomers.

Gauguin submitted eighteen canvases. There were works by Pissarro, his son, Lucien Pissarro, Berthe Morisot, Guillaumin, and a newcomer, Odilon Redon. The presence of the latter marked the disintegration of the group. Redon already represented symbolism, which was trying to assert its position. The public was drawn in by works that made them guffaw, such as one canvas that has since become famous, and is today justifiably regarded as a masterpiece— *La Grande Jatte* by Seurat. Signac was painting in the same style. This was pointillism, the last incarnation of Impressionism! Gauguin, however, did not allow himself to be attracted by this new aesthetic form. Once again he fled, and took refuge in Brittany where he could live cheaply, and where the solitude finally gave him the opportunity to face his problems as a painter.

His mastery was now undeniable; he knew how to play with light and colour in order to build up a landscape. His palette had brightened without attaining the sunlit brilliance of Claude Monet. He had learned to arrange his subject in a poetic and evocative manner. But a certain style imposes a certain way of seeing things. As an Impressionist, his vision remained realistic. He might use every possible freedom in his work, and yet in the end his painting would still do no more than express a fleeting moment in the landscape that had inspired him. Gauguin found such limitations intolerable. Landscape was insufficient for him. He dreamed of expressing other things, of portraying his agonies, his dreams and his ideals; he was thinking ahead to a form of painting that addressed the heart as well as the eyes. What signifiance did the pointillist revolution hold for him? It was no more than a superficial technique! The effect was similar, whether dots or colour harmonised or contrasted, and the new school simply amounted to a different but equivalent expression of the same landscape. This, at least was Gauguin's view. From an objective viewpoint, however, Seurat had opened the way to an intellectual and scientific form of painting. He had instinctively refused to put a sensual feeling in concrete terms. He had studied optical and visual phenomena. Following the theories of the German, Helmholtz, and Chevreul, the Frenchman, he determined to use pure colours, and restricted himself to the primary ones of blue, red and yellow. Instead of using green, for example, he placed minute dots of blue and yellow next to each other – from a distance the eye effects the optical mixture, thus giving the illusion of green. The whole canvas was treated in the 'needle point' way, and the composition accordingly had to follow certain major geometric patterns. Seurat was the first major example of a rationalised form of art taken to extremes, typical of the schizoid personality, and which was to lead up to the later pure abstract work around 1925 of the Dutchman, Mondrian.

LITTLE BRETON GIRLS IN A ROUND DANCE. 1888.
Private Collection, Scotland.

Gauguin who had fought for the title of painter, and was no longer
an amateur and a beginner, now coolly observed the rise of this
new school, but made no attempt to join it. He already had a feeling
that his own personal truth lay elsewhere, though he did not yet
know where. It still remained for him to discover it. The time he
spent in Brittany was to help him to do this.

THE FREEDOM OF THE POOR

When a rich man who lacks for nothing comes into an important
sum of money, he invests it, saves and increases his capital. When

LES ALYSCAMPS. 1888.
Louvre, Paris.

a man who is short of money benefits from such a fortunate event, he usually settles his debts, and then loses no time in spending the money, either to meet urgent necessities or simply to satisfy certain long-felt yearnings. Gauguin had always acted in this way, and continued to do so for the rest of his life. This natural disposition explains why he was always short of money.

It is probably more a matter of temperament than of wealth – pessimists hoard money for fear of what may happen tomorrow; optimists, on the other hand, spend because they have confidence in the future and Gauguin was one of the latter. Even in his most prosperous period, Gauguin never saved, and when chance events on the stock-exchange handsomely augmented his earnings at the bank, he built up a collection of paintings for his own pleasure. His good taste made this whim into an excellent investment and the works which were subsequently sold helped him and his wife out of a corner on numerous occasions. And even then he was most reluctant to part with them! 'I value my two Cézannes which are very rare of their kind, for he did not finish many and one day they will be worth a great deal.' 'Rather sell the Degas drawing ... I have left the paintings in Denmark, and the way things are going, I shall soon have none left at all!'

To others he appeared extravagant, and Gauguin was in fact egoistic, optimistic and impulsive, and remained so always. In May he made his first sale for a long while, and received 250 francs from Félix Bracquemond, the engraver, for a canvas he had exhibited at the last Impressionist exhibition. He immediately decided to go and work in Brittany, at Pont-Aven, where he had been assured by other artists that one could live 'for nothing' – 60 francs a month at the Pension Gloanec. His luck seemed to be changing.

Furthermore, Bracquemond, an old friend of Manet, who held an important post at the Sèvres pottery works, put him in touch with the potter, Ernest Chaplet. From the beginning of the winter Gauguin would be able to go and work there, and would share the profits with Bracquemond. His future was now taken care of. Gauguin dreamed of the peace awaiting him in Brittany, and prepared for his departure. For a while he thought of taking his son Clovis with him, but he then thought better of it and decided to leave him in the boarding school he was already attending, which Gauguin had been paying for so sporadically that occasionally his sister Marie would have to step in and settle the arrears.

The rough and primitive character of the Breton atmosphere, its landscape and its people were exactly what Gauguin had been hoping for. In Brittany he was to find his way again, to succeed in controlling his own originality and to create his first masterpieces. His four main stays there were of major importance for his work.

The first time was when he spent the summer of 1886 there and met Emile Bernard. His second stay was in the middle of 1888 on his return from Martinique and ended with his departure for Arles, where he joined Van Gogh. He completed several major canvases there, among them the first masterpieces of synthetism, *Vision after the Sermon* (page 49) and *Portrait of Madeleine Bernard* (page 57).

He returned to Brittany the following year and spent the winter of 1889–90 at Le Pouldu. This was a period of intense creative activity, which produced such important works as *The Yellow Christ* (page 104), *La Belle Angèle* (page 77) and *Bonjour Monsieur Gauguin* (pages 89, 93), among others. He was in Pont-Aven and Le Pouldu once more during the summer of 1894, with Annah, the Javanese girl, between his two voyages to Tahiti, and broke an ankle during a brawl with some Concarneau sailors.

THE DISCOVERY OF BRITTANY

Pont-Aven with its present-day population of eighteen hundred inhabitants is a village at the tip of Brittany, on the south coast of Finistère, ten miles east of Concarneau. The countryside is austere with gently undulating fields and orchards enclosed by hedges. The moss-covered grey stone walls of the houses with their slate roofs add to the melancholy appearance. The tiny harbour is not directly on the sea but at the mouth of the river Aven, whence its name. Higher up, following the course of the river, edged with poplars,

OLD MAIDS OF ARLES. 1888.
Art Institute of Chicago.

there are a few windmills. It is a little tourist spot that is overrun
by Anglo-Saxon and Scandinavian artists. Americans were already
going there in the middle of the last century. The artist Jobbé-Duval
used to go there regularly from 1860 onwards, and it was he that
gave his friend the address of the Pension Gloanec.

Gauguin was being economical and took an attic room. The comfort was only relative, but the food abundant, and for him this was
relaxation, almost a holiday – but a working holiday. He immediately
began to draw without a stop, before daring to start to paint. He
set off in the morning with his materials on his back and did not

72

return until nightfall. In the evening all the guests ate together around the inn's large table. Charles Laval, who had worked in the studio of the great officially recognized painter, Bonnat, was suffering from ill health that had been made worse by all kinds of excesses; Granchi-Taylor from Lyon had, like Gauguin, fled from the stock-exchange. Emile Bernard had made the acquaintance of Granchi-Taylor and Schuffenecker, who had come to join Gauguin in Brittany. He passed through Pont-Aven, but despite the attempts of their mutual friends he would have nothing to do with Gauguin that year. The latter refused to see him, and when they finally met he made no attempt at any conversation with the young artist, who was then painting in the pointillist style of Seurat.

In Paris Gauguin had felt ill at ease in the company of the pioneers of Impressionism. Amidst the group of artists at Pont-Aven, he was looked upon as a revolutionary painter. The majority consisted in fact of artists who belonged to the Academy. He had now found himself, and displayed exaggerated confidence in his own personality. He would hold forth at table, severely criticizing the paintings of his neighbours, and did not scorn to act the master. In addition to this, he had been seen swimming across the estuary – he went bathing in the nude, and in a nearby fencing-school he had proved himself to be a dangerous duelling partner. All this added even further, if not to his prestige, at least to his reputation.

'I am working a great deal here and with some success. I am respected as the best painter at Pont-Aven, although admittedly this does not make me any richer,' he wrote to Mette in July. 'Still, it gives me a respectable reputation, and everyone here is arguing over my opinions ...'

Strangely enough, it was the subjects that he discovered in Brittany that determined the development of his style. The firm, clear outlines of the white head-dresses of the Breton women were to light up a number of his paintings (page 101). As their shapes grew increasingly sharply defined, the details of the countryside began to stand out in corresponding manner. At first Gauguin remained faithful to the true colours of the costumes, then he exaggerated them, painting them in terms of pure colour. He was moving away from Impressionism with its play of light, which tended to drown nature in an overpowering almost monochrome tonality. His landscapes are no longer clouded in a dim and indistinct haze, like someone blinded by the glaring sun. The painter now imposes the clarity of his own vision on their design and composition. The colour has

WASHERWOMEN. 1888.
Charles Durand-Ruel Collection, Paris.

become more vivid, and ventures at contrasts, which are barely softened by the individual brushstrokes.

During this first season in Brittany, there was a crystallisation in Gauguin's own particular pictorial method. The treatment of the skies was still somewhat indefinite in relation to the sharp relief of the landscapes, but the intentions of the artist were being made manifest with undeniable strength. When he took up his brushes to start work on a landscape or a peasant scene Gauguin already had a clear idea of what he wished to express and the features he wished to emphasize. In this way he extolled the nostalgic poetry of a countryside that corresponded so well with his present mood.

September came, and winter was approaching. He began to think of leaving, and impressed upon his memory, with the colours he applied to the canvas, the details of the sombre but invigorating countryside and the taciturn, stubborn, yet pure and sincere character of the people that was one with the land that belonged to them. The ruggedness of Brittany and its backwardness, bred of isolation, made Gauguin move towards simplicity and return to a form of primitivism. He purified his palette, limiting himself to the primary colours, and felt no reluctance in abandoning the aims so dear to the Impressionists in order to synthesize vision. 'Synthesis' was soon to become a byword and a great success in Paris.

WOMAN MINDING COWS. 1889.
Ny Carlsberg Glyptothek, Copenhagen.

Gauguin left Pont-Aven on 13th November and moved into small lodgings at 257 rue Lecourbe in Paris, which the ever faithful Schuffenecker had found for him. He sold a small Jongkind from his collection for 350 francs, in order to pay the arrears on the school fees for his son, Clovis, and despite the constant colds from which he suffered, it was with great enthusiasm that he began working for Ernest Chaplet, the potter.

The objects he turned, modelled and decorated, were neither pottery, nor sculpture, but a mixture of the two. He attempted to respect the classic shape of the pot and the vase, incorporating into it Breton scenes and decorative relief motifs, often separating the different glazes by an outline in relief, a sort of cloisonné effect like that of the Chinese potters, using the technique which in enamelling is called 'champlevé' in Limoges. Occasionally recollections of Peruvian pottery gave his work an exotic quality. This style was equivalent to the one he later developed in painting in 1888 at Pont-Aven and which was to be named 'the cloisonnist school'.

His friends were very enthusiastic over the first attempts, Bracquemond most of all, since he had been the one to start him off on this new venture. 'Schuffenecker says,' Gauguin wrote to Mette, 'that these are masterpieces, and so does the potter, but they are probably too artistic to sell. However he does say that if this idea could be accepted by the exhibition of industrial arts, it would be a huge success. Meanwhile my entire wardrobe is in pawn, and I cannot even go and see people.'

Success was not so quick in coming. There was to be another winter of poverty, and to make matters worse a twenty-eight days' stay in hospital, for his constant colds had brought about an inflammation of the tonsils, and it had become necessary to remove them. To make up for this, Gauguin did go out, contrary to what he wrote his wife, to the Nouvelle Athènes café, where he met Degas. The latter invited him home to talk, and in this way a protective friendship grew up that never weakened.

LA BELLE ANGÈLE. 1889.
Louvre, Paris.

During that winter Gauguin talked a lot but painted comparatively little. His material position was hardly encouraging. 'I have suffered extreme poverty ... You become accustomed to it, and with the right attitude, you end up by laughing at it. But the terrible thing is the way it stops you from working, from developing your intellectual faculties ... On the other hand, it is perfectly true that suffering sharpens one's genius,' he was to write late in his *Cahier pour ma fille Aline* (Notebook for my daughter Aline).

A CRAZY ESCAPADE TO PANAMA AND MARTINIQUE

Success being slow to reward his efforts, Gauguin now allowed himself to be taken up by the idea of going to Panama. His aim was twofold – to earn a lot of money in a short time by working in one of the gangs that had begun to dig the canal, and with this money to be able to paint for several months without any worries. His brother-in-law, Juan Uribe, had gone to Panama. Gauguin had turned down an offer to go and work with him on the grounds that the conditions Uribe had proposed were unsatisfactory, but he was hoping to be able to rely on his help in this foreign country. Charles Laval was to accompany him, impelled as much by friendship as by the glowing accounts of the paradise that awaited them there.

It was a long voyage and Gauguin was somewhat nervous. He took the precaution of giving his wife power of attorney, as beneficiary in his uncle Isidore's inheritance, in the event of the latter's death. He abandoned Clovis at his school, instructing Mette 'to repatriate him'. The phrase is significant and displays a cavalier attitude.

Nevertheless he was dreaming of a better future. Carried away by the false grandeur of his schemes, he forgot his bitter feelings: 'One of these days I hope we shall be reunited ...' His letters became almost tender. Mette came rushing over from Copenhagen in order to embrace him before his departure, and in order to take back little Clovis.

The two artists left Paris on 9th April and set sail on the 10th from Saint-Nazaire. After a difficult crossing they reached Colon, and instead of the paradise they had expected they found a hell of humid heat; it was the rainy season, and they found themselves in the midst of a horde of adventurers. Speculation was at its height, and the artist's brother-in-law, Juan Uribe, opened neither his heart nor his wallet. Storming against him, Gauguin was reduced to working as a labourer, while Charles Laval went about canvassing for commissions for routine portraits. A high percentage of the labour force was periodically carried off by epidemics of fever, and would constantly be replaced, until supplies were held up, when the men would be dismissed without any notice.

Laval, seriously ill after an attempt at suicide, and Gauguin who was now thoroughly sick at heart, pooled their savings and set sail for Martinique. Once in St Pierre on Martinique they would have been wildly enthusiastic, had it not been for the complete depletion of their funds. Gauguin wrote to Paris, to Schuffenecker in particular, in the hope that one of his canvases might have been sold, and asked for the proceeds to be sent to him without delay.

The countryside visible from the hut they had rented, the beauty of the women, whose skins ranged in colour from deep ebony to white, and the vivid colours of their clothes, dazzled the two friends, and they set to work energetically. For them it was a revelation of the magic of colour in all its brilliance. Impressionism served as an adequate means of expressing their wonder, but they soon became aware of its limitations. Appropriate to the delicate light and shade of Western Europe, here it seemed affected, and incapable of fully rendering the intensities of contrast that blaze in the tropics.

Laval and Gauguin worked side by side, with virtually the same approach, to the extent that today practically all the canvases painted by Laval in Martinique have disappeared from the market – they are signed Paul Gauguin!

In spite of being short of money, their life would have been quite tolerable, had not Gauguin now fallen seriously ill with fever, accompanied by dysentery. 'At the moment my body looks like a skeleton and I can barely whisper . . . My stomach has caused me agonies. The little that I do eat at present gives me excruciating liver pains . . . The last of my money has gone on medicines and doctors' fees ... I am in a native hut, lying exhausted on a mattress of seaweed, without the necessary cash to take me back to France ...' During this same month of August 1887, he asked Schuffenecker, 'I implore you ... do the impossible and send me two to three hundred francs immediately. Sell my pictures for forty or fifty francs apiece, sell all I possess at any ridiculous price, but I must get out of here, otherwise I shall die like a dog!' But mail took a month to get to France.

Gauguin, who had once been a seaman, now signed on as a sailor on a sailing-ship bound for Europe, and left Laval behind.

STILL LIFE WITH JAPANESE PRINT. 1889.
Mr and Mrs Henry Ittleson Jr. Collection, New York.

LANDSCAPE WITH PINK TREE, 1888.
Private Collection, Paris.

THEO VAN GOGH, THE ARTISTS' PATRON

Paul Gauguin arrived in Paris looking pale, thin and ill at the end
of November 1887 when the weather was cold. Ever faithful, 'Good
old Schuff', took him to the little house where he lived at 29 rue
Boulard, not far from Montparnasse. He had his own studio, which
he willingly let Gauguin use. Thus fed and housed, Gauguin slowly
regained his health in the warm atmosphere of this friendly home.
He had lost nothing of his reserved air or his disdainful manner,

which were emphasized by the hardships he had recently endured. He was regarded as proud and very much aware of his own superiority, superiority that was still open to some dispute.

But when he unpacked and showed his paintings of Martinique, his friends realized that here was a contribution of something entirely new to the art of their time. It was a revelation not merely in the brightly coloured, exotic subjects, the landscapes with their unknown trees and the black, Venus-like figures draped in their gaudy finery; it was the whole atmosphere that was new, a kind of poetry, an emotion that Schuffenecker and Theo van Gogh found fascinating and disconcerting.

Gauguin had got to know the brothers, Theo and Vincent van Gogh at the art dealer's, Boussod-Valadon, on the Boulevard Montmartre, where Theo worked, and a few of Vincent's paintings were exhibited. A bond of mutual sympathy rapidly grew up between them. Vincent invited Gauguin to take part in an exhibition to be held at Portier's in Montmartre, in rue Lepic, and Theo followed the development of his brother's friend with growing interest. Not being in a position to persuade his employers to 'commit themselves and take a risk' for the artists he liked, he helped them himself by buying as many of their canvases as he could afford. This was part of a grand dream he cherished together with his brother, of an artists' mutual aid association. Theo van Gogh bought three of Gauguin's Martinique paintings for 900 francs and also organized an exhibition for him. Together with the proceeds of the few ceramics that had already been sold, this was almost a fortune in Gauguin's eyes, and would at least have assured him some respite, if it had not been for the many debts and obligations he had. He sent 100 francs to his wife, and settled the arrears in fees that were still owing at Clovis' school, and then prepared to leave once again for Pont-Aven.

His exhibition achieved no more than a mild success in the public eye, and none whatever on the commercial level, but it aroused controversial discussion in artistic circles. Such discussions were evidence that Gauguin's painting had now been noticed, and the artist found criticism stimulating. There was no longer any doubt as to his originality, his style was rapidly developing, and he now needed to work continually in order to keep pace with his ideas.

Before going back to Brittany, he was confronted with a fresh domestic issue. His wife, who had learned of the sums of money he had recently received, now tried to entice him back to Denmark. But something in Gauguin's heart had snapped. 'In order to preserve my moral strength, I have gradually suppressed the tender feelings of my heart,' he wrote. He also realized that if he were to see his children again he would only suffer all the more at the separation that would follow. Finally, 'the money for the fare would be enough for me to live on for three months in Brittany'. He wished to paint and fled, perhaps in a cowardly way, from domestic scenes. He arrived in Pont-Aven under a dismal sky in February 1888.

THE LESSON OF HOKUSAI

In his new Breton paintings, Gauguin was to follow literally the advice he had given Schuffenecker in that patronising tone he customarily now used with him.

The idea had not sprung out of thin air. The whole group at Pont-Aven looked upon the Japanese print as an example and an authority. They were all captivated by the expressive boldness of the stylisations, the purity of line and the powerful and dynamic outline of the shapes; here was a process that could be put to use. All that was needed was to adapt it to a western style. The current work of the Japanese was accepted in their own country. Why should European artists not try to do the same? It did not follow that the Parisian public would reject it out of hand. Doubtless neither Gauguin, nor Emile Bernard, whom he was to meet again and with whom he finally made friends, approached the subject in this rational way. But they moved more or less consciously towards the same attitude.

Vincent van Gogh had been the instigator of the interest in this subject. Behind his *Portrait du Père Tanguy*, dated 1887, he had placed a whole collection of Japanese prints representing geishas and warriors. At the beginning of 1888, before leaving for Arles, he had

WILLOW TREES. 1889.
National Gallery, Oslo.

painted a whole series of pictures in the Japanese manner–an *Actor* in the style of Kesai Yeisen, and especially *The Bridge* after Hiroshige. Van Gogh had been buying these prints for three sous from the dealer, Bing, and selling them for five. As early as 1883 there had been an important exhibition of Japanese prints at the Petit Gallery, and a number of writers had expressed their enthusiasm for Japanese art. The Goncourt brothers later published, among others, a study on Hokusai.

The characteristic style of Japanese prints stems from a particular technique combined with masterly virtuosity. The wood is cut with the grain, making the material resistant, and the grain in the wood enlivens the flat tints and creates moiré effects that are exploited to the full. The cost involved, as well as the difficulty of registering the impressions of the different blocks when it comes to printing, limits the number of colours used. Finally the nature of the wood itself dictates the technique, and results in simple, fine, spare strokes that have to compensate for the economy in colour.

In the landscapes one finds large monochrome areas, whilst splashes of colour are further heightened by outlines in black. These prints are beautifully composed and succeed in conveying movement within an atmosphere of calm and serenity, and yet retain a plastic 'stability'. It was also their exoticism that attracted western artists. Prints by Hokusai and Hiroshige now began to appear pinned up in the background of a number of Gauguin's canvases, like in the *Still Life* of 1889 (page 80). It is particularly interesting to compare some of the famous prints, as has been done in a remarkable study by Madame Yvonne Thirion, with the canvases Gauguin painted during those years; certain similarities are so striking that it seems quite clear that he must have been familiar with these prints and did not hesitate to draw inspiration from them. The composition of *The Wave*, 1888, and *The Boat*, painted in the same year, is like that of Hiroshige prints. The two men fighting in *Vision after the Sermon* (page 49) are in the same attitudes as Hiroshige's warriors, the *Little Dogs* are reminiscent of *Cats* by Kuniyoshi, and some of the Breton women have the priestly, dramatic poses of Utamaro's figures.

CHILD WITH BIB. 1895 (?)
Private Collection.

But this minor revolution did not come about lightly, and it caused some heated conflicts at Pont-Aven.

AT PONT-AVEN WITH EMILE BERNARD

Gauguin had had a photograph taken of himself in profile. The curves of his aquiline nose are echoed in the lines of his drooping moustache and his jutting chin, and give him an air of authority and

NEAR THE CLIFF. 1888.
Private Collection, U.S.A.

self-satisfaction. He is dressed so simply that his clothes look modern –a jacket without lapels over a turtle-necked sweater and a white shirt. The cap looks like a halo crowning the new-found prestige of the master of the new school. There is also a group photograph that gives a comical and old-fashioned impression of the atmosphere at the Pension Gloanec, in front of which it was taken. All the 'gentlemen' together with their 'ladies' and the proprietress had posed in front of the dreary façade of this country inn. The casual attire of the men, and the bizarre variety in their head-gear are in striking contrast to the severity of their wives' black dresses. The only bright touches are provided by the head-dress of 'la Belle Angèle', and Madeleine Bernard's full-skirted dress. Gauguin, right at the back, with his moustache and solemn look, a straw-hat tilted back on his head, is surrounded by his bearded acolytes, Emile Bernard and Paul Sérusier, whilst a few idlers and outsiders are casually sitting on the edge of the pavement.

Spurred on by rivalry, some of the group relied on boldness to match the experience of the others, and developments were rapidly to be seen. There was to be some argument as to the respective parts played by Emile Bernard and Gauguin in the birth of the Pont-Aven school. Certain ideas were in the air, and painting the same subjects, as they did, working close to each other and towards the same end, it was inevitable that at a given moment the two men should meet and their styles intermingle. Neither man felt any resentment at this, since they were now friends, but later Gauguin was to harbour a feeling of bitterness at the way in which 'little Bernard' had in 1891 claimed to be the originator of the movement.

At this point it would be as well to define the terms cloisonnism and synthetism. Cloisonnism derives from a technical process – it is taken from the French word 'cloisonner' meaning to partition – and consists of separating off clearly defined shapes and different colours by a strong outline.

The synthetist school corresponds to an intellectual attitude. By presenting shapes in a 'cloisonnist' or 'separated' manner, the artists 'synthesised' the subject. They unified the various component parts into one single, coloured whole, thus establishing an aesthetic and intellectual synthesis. The entire picture became a homogenous synthesis of the elements that were integrated into it.

After his first months of solitude – 'No one to exchange ideas with ...' – Gauguin had watched the first 'black painters', the conventional artists arrive, with whom he did not associate. Then the friends, the members of the old set, had come. There were Charles Laval, ever faithful, Henri Moret, a newcomer, Paul Sérusier, and

BONJOUR MONSIEUR GAUGUIN. 1889.
Count Yvan N. Podgoursky Collection, San Antonio, Texas, U.S.A.

finally Emile Bernard, whom Gauguin had met a number of times in Paris during the previous winter, and whom he now welcomed warmly. The more the 'set' grew the more it pleased him, for he was after all the leader of this school, and the number of people surrounding him added to his prestige. Sérusier later recounted: 'This little group lived separately and ate separately, and had nothing to do with the other people staying at the Pension Gloanec, with the students from the Beaux-Arts and from the Julian Academy, or with the English or the Americans.'

At sunrise, Bernard and Gauguin would go and settle down in front of the same 'subjects', exchanging ideas, and each influencing the other. Gauguin, who was initially less talented, now had far greater experience as a painter and possessed the maturity that comes with age. Bernard, however, though young and impulsive, had an intellectual approach, and he was able to express what Gauguin could only confusedly feel. He clarified his ideas for him, telling him of Van Gogh's thoughts on the use of pure colour, the simplification of shapes, and the symbolic value of a single form silhouetted against the light. They were painting almost the same pictures – the peasant women in Emile Bernard's *Breton Women in the Meadow* are remarkably similar to those in Gauguin's *Vision after the Sermon* (page 49). The outline and stylization of the head-dresses are curiously alike. The dark tone on which the canvas is built up, recurs again to emphasize the shape of the background and make it stand out, almost in relief. In *Pont-Aven* by Bernard there are the same horizontal rhythms as in Gauguin's *Landscape with Pink Tree* (page 81), and in both of them the slanting line of a tree trunk is the only thing that breaks up the calm and enlivens the composition. The white splash of the geese in the one corresponds to that of the sheep in the other, but Emile Bernard's treatment is much drier, and his composition far more rigid and intellectual, whereas Gauguin has worked eagerly but patiently at his idea, covering the surface with closely serried, determined though modulated strokes, that give a dazzling effect to the whole. His lines are more supple, and often undulating, not like the frenzied undulations of Van Gogh, but always retaining a measured, almost musical rhythm. The colours are sometimes broken up, in order to produce contrasts in a close harmony that is brilliant, though never explosive.

That same summer, Gauguin and Bernard both did a *Portrait of Madeleine Bernard* (page 57). The young artist's mother and sister had come to join him. Madeleine, who was freer in her conversation than in her behaviour, would chat with her brother's friends. She was passionate to the point of romanticism and Gauguin responded to the young girl's charm, though she was engaged to Charles Laval. With this model before them, the two artists suddenly revealed different views – the brother's uncomplicated approach outlined the features of the face, widening the narrow slit of the two dark eyes, and surrounded her with the thick mass of hair, placing her squarely in the picture against a scene that was also expressed in clearly defined cloisonnist terms. By contrast, Gauguin timidly returned to an outdated, almost Impressionist style, presenting his model in semi-profile, with a suggestion of graceful movement. Everything, from the tint of the outlines, the print that appears on the upper part of the picture, the dark splash of the dress, the jacket draped around the shoulders, that lights up the face with its bright mass, down to the position of the arm and hand, which is the centre of the composition, drawing the attention back to the sidelong glance, the humorous nose and the ironic mouth, all these details conspire to emphasize the charm of the model, and the tenderness with which these are portrayed betrays the artist's feelings.

This strictly platonic adventure ended with the summer. Madeleine's parents forbade her to write to Gauguin. Gauguin sent her a letter as a form of farewell, containing somewhat cynical advice, tinged with irony, on how to succeed in life. In December 1888 he sent her a ceramic as a souvenir through Emile Bernard: 'At Goupil's there is a little unpolished pot with a design of a bird on a blue-green background. Accept it from me. It is for Madeleine. Silence is the order of the day, but I hope that she will sometimes think of her elder brother when she fills it with flowers. It is a rather rough thing, but I put a lot of myself into it . . . The pot is quite cool now, yet it

CARICATURE PORTRAIT OF GAUGUIN. 1889.
National Gallery, Washington.

BONJOUR MONSIEUR GAUGUIN. 1889.
Prague Museum.

was capable of withstanding a temperature of 1600 degrees. Looking at it, one might imagine some of that warmth in the maker.'

At the end of the summer Gauguin resumed his correspondence with Schuffenecker: ' All the Americans are raging against Impressionism, so that I was forced to threaten them with a fight, and now we have peace' ... 'My latest work is going well and I believe you might detect in it a special note or rather an affirmation of my recent searching, or a SYNTHESIS OF A FORM AND A COLOUR WITHOUT EITHER ONE BEING DOMINANT.'

Well aware of the importance of his progress, he felt that he was approaching his goal: 'I am very satisfied with my studies of Pont-Aven. Degas is buying the one of two Breton peasant-women at Avins *(Two Breton Women at Avins)*. I consider this the highest form of flattery, for you know I place the greatest confidence in Degas' judgment – besides, from a commercial point of view it is a very good beginning.' But Gauguin's admiration for Degas did not extend to the point of imitation: 'I have just done some nudes which you will like. And there is nothing of Degas about them.'

In Paris Sérusier was showing all his friends the rough sketch painted on the edge of the Bois d'amour, (a local beauty spot) an example of synthetism, which Maurice Denis, Bonnard, Vuillard, K. X. Roussel, Paul Ranson, pupils of the Julian Academy, christened the *Talisman*. It is a small work, rippling with light, with trees that are really green and shadows of a deep blue; the treatment – all in vertical strokes – is both rigid and free. This modest study with its poetic power was to become a symbol to the small group. 'In this way we knew that every work of art was a transposition, and a caricature, a passionate equivalent of a disappointed emotion,' Maurice Denis wrote later.

VAN GOGH'S INVITATION

Winter was drawing near. Gauguin was trying to find the money to leave and answer the call of Van Gogh, who was insistently begging him to come and join him at Arles. In October Theo van Gogh bought 'three hundred francs worth of pottery' from him with the obvious intention of enabling him to leave Pont-Aven and pay his fare. But a few days later on 16th October, Gauguin wrote to Schuffenecker: 'You know what a sucker I am for paying my debts as soon as I have a bit of money. Well, I have paid the doctor and some of what I owe Marie-Jeanne [of the Pension Gloanec] without stopping to count, and now I don't have enough for the fare. Do me a favour and go and see Van Gogh *immediately* and arrange for him to send me fifty francs. Send me a telegram right away.'

Vincent van Gogh's friendship with Gauguin dated back to their first meeting two years previously at the Boussod-Valadon gallery. Since he had arrived in Paris, within a period of barely two years Van Gogh had developed with astonishing speed, taking the achievements of the Impressionists in his stride, discovering oriental art, and being entirely enslaved by the light. His brother, Theo, who had been in Paris a long time, was a valuable guide to him, since he would give him excellent advice, and was, moreover, always ready to help him. Van Gogh had settled in Paris; he was able to do a lot of work, owing to the modest monthly allowance which his brother paid him regularly. Van Gogh was five years younger than Gauguin and sold no more than he did. Since he had a huge house in Arles at his disposal, why should Gauguin not take advantage of this? By sharing their loneliness and wretchedness, they would lead a better life and they could form the first embryo of a future artists' colony.

Theo, who supplied the money, had been willing to pay for the additional cost of Gauguin's presence there from the beginning of June, in return for about one canvas a month. It is interesting to note that Gauguin, who, one would have thought, would have jumped at the opportunity, was unenthusiastic about the invitation. Was it that he thought Theo was being calculating? In July he agreed unreservedly to a sale that would enable him to pay off his debts and leave Pont-Aven. Van Gogh was becoming impatient. He already saw his studio in the south as an idyllic community of artists living together in harmony, and regarded it with the same idealism that had caused him to go and preach the Gospel to the miners of the Borinage district. To hell with debts – let Gauguin leave his paintings as security, 'and if they don't accept them, just leave your debts without the paintings as a security' ... 'I had to do just the same in order to come to Paris ...' he wrote to his brother Theo.

Vincent had a somewhat romantic approach to this idea of living together. He bowed to Gauguin as to his master. During the course of the summer while they were waiting to come together, they exchanged self-portraits. Gauguin described his own in this letter to Schuffenecker, dated 8th October:

BE AMOROUS AND YOU WILL BE HAPPY. 1889.
Private Collection, U.S.A.

'I have done a portrait of myself for Vincent, for which he asked
me. I think it is one of the best things I have done: absolutely incomprehensible (Imagine!) – it is so abstract. First a bandit's head,
a Jean Valjean (*Les Miserables*), likewise a personification of a dis-
credited impressionist painter, eternally shouldering the burden of
the world. The drawing is something quite unusual, completely
abstract. The eyes, mouth and nose are like the flowers on a Persian carpet, also representing the symbolic side. The colour is a colour

ONDINE. 1889.
Mr and Mrs Powell Jones Collection, Gates Mills, Ohio, U.S.A.

far from nature – imagine something like pottery all twisted by the
heat of the furnace! All the reds, the purples streaked with flames
like a furnace blazing in the eyes, reflecting the mental battles of
the artist. The whole against a chrome background, scattered with
childish posies.'

How can one best describe this work and the purpose behind it?
For Vincent it was 'a prisoner. There is not a hint of gaiety . . . he
has the look of a sick man in this tortured portrait'. These at least

are the impressions he divulged to his brother. To Gauguin he wrote: 'I have done a painting especially for the room you will have, *A poet's garden*. In the communal gardens there are plants and bushes that make one think of the landscapes associated with Botticelli, Giotto, Petrarch, Dante and Boccaccio ... I wanted to paint this garden in such a way that it would evoke both the ancient poet who lived here (or rather in Avignon), namely Petrarch, as well as the new poet to live here–Paul Gauguin.'

Van Gogh would not accept Gauguin's self-portrait which he found too fine compared with his own, saying that his brother would be happy to take it against the cost of a month's living expenses.

Gauguin travelled to Arles by train, arriving in the night of 19th to 20th October 1888. A major chapter in the history of modern art was about to unfurl. The clash between two outstanding personalities was imminent, and out of this clash was to come the twofold spark of genius. It was to leave Van Gogh morally broken, but with his talent intact; Gauguin was to emerge disturbed and unsettled. But the fire born of this impact was to shed a light for each man on to his own real nature. This episode has been recounted in the numerous monographs devoted to each of the two artists. Strangely enough, the version Gauguin gave of it after a long silence is accurate, and Van Gogh never referred to it afterwards. So let us see what Gauguin had to say about it, and simply restrict ourselves to commenting on his statements:

'Readers of the *Mercure* will have gathered from a letter of Vincent's published a few years ago, how he insisted on my coming to Arles to carry out his idea of founding a studio, of which I was to be the head. At that time I was working at Pont-Aven in Brittany, and it was either that the studies I had begun there held me to the place, or that I had some vague intuition, sensing something that was not quite normal, in any case I held back for a long time before allowing myself to be finally overcome by Vincent's sincere overtures of friendship and setting off to join him.

'I arrived in Arles in the middle of the night, and waited until daybreak in an all-night café. The owner looked at me and cried:

'You're his friend. I recognize you.' It is easy enough to explain the man's outburst. I had sent Vincent a portrait of myself, and Vincent had shown it to him, saying that this was a friend of his who was shortly to join him.

'At a reasonable hour I went along to wake Vincent. The day was spent in getting me settled in, and a great deal of chatter, and a walk to show me the beauty of Arles and its girls—whom, by the way, I could not get very enthusiastic about.

'The following morning we set to work, he continuing with his, and I starting afresh. I must tell you that I have never had that uninhibited facility of some who can simply rely on the tips of their brushes. They can get off a train, take up their palette, and in no time at all dash off an impression of sunshine. As soon as it is dry, it gets sent off to Luxembourg, signed Carolus-Durand . . .

'Wherever I am, I need an incubation period, each time I need to get to know the plants and the trees, in short the whole of nature —which is so varied and so capricious, and seems to make itself deliberately elusive and difficult to grasp.

'Thus it took me several weeks to become aware of the bitter flavour of Arles and its surroundings. This did not prevent us from working hard, especially Vincent. Between the two of us, the one a volcano, and the other boiling, too, but inwardly, there was a kind of battle that was brewing.'

THE CLASH OF TWO GENIUSES

The period of Gauguin's stay with Van Gogh can be divided into two parts. There was the initial period of making contact. Gauguin, not without some reservations, thought it would be possible to lead a communal life, and even to invite friends to join them. He wrote to Emile Bernard: 'Van Gogh [he was referring to Theo] has pre-pared the way, and I believe it could be possible for all the gifted artists in our group to manage in this way . . . If you could come here, life would not be too difficult. I have gone into the question of money and we can live quite cheaply by doing what I intend to

BRETON CHILDHOOD. 1889.
Private Collection.

do from tomorrow onwards (doing our own cooking at home).' This
was in November. As far as Vincent was concerned, he had welcomed Gauguin as the head of the Studio, and as a master, in the
full glow of his prestige as the leader of synthetism, and was now
bent on following the advice of Gauguin to paint in a cloisonnist
style. The outcome of this was a series of paintings which are neither
among the better paintings of Van Gogh, nor are they good imi-
tations of Gauguin. In this category, the *Portrait of Madame Roulin
with her Baby* is frankly bad. The *Dance Hall*, the *Amphitheatre
at Arles* and the *Walk in Arles* are questionable. Van Gogh was
trying to force himself to paint in flat tones, to use outlines, and his
painting became somewhat cold and stiff, except when he gave way
to his own temperament and returned to his swirling brushstrokes.

HARVEST IN BRITTANY. 1889.
Courtauld Institute, London.

During the second part of his stay, Gauguin became irritated by the sentimentality of his host, by his untidiness, and perhaps by the fact that he had not succeeded in making a disciple of him. 'It's odd that Vincent sees this place in terms of Daumier, whereas on the contrary I see it in terms of Puvis' [de Chavannes] subjects in Japanese colours.' The two friends went to Montpelier to visit the museum containing the Bruyas collection. It was here that Gauguin discovered the famous painting, *Bonjour Monsieur Courbet* which he took up the following year in Brittany, producing his own version under the title, *Bonjour Monsieur Gauguin*. Their differing reactions to these works revealed how far apart they stood. It was after this discussion that he wrote to Emile Bernard: 'I feel quite out of my element in Arles, everything seems so petty and shabby to me, both the scenery and the people. On the whole Vincent and I do not agree about most things, particularly as far as painting is concerned. He admires Daumier, Daubigny, Ziem and the great Rousseau, all of whom I cannot abide. On the other hand, he detests Ingres, Raphael and Degas, all the people I admire. For my part, I say, "Right you are, Captain" just to keep the peace. He likes my paintings very much, but when I am working on them, he always points out that this or that is wrong. He is a romantic, whereas I tend to be more of a primitive. As far as colour is concerned, he goes into the chance effects of paint, whereas I detest his fiddling about, etc . . .' This was written in December. For his part, Van Gogh had given up painting in the cloisonnist style and was no longer trying to master the principles of synthetism. With his painting of *The Red Vines* (which today is the pride of the Pushkin Museum) he once again returned to his swirling paint and parallel brushstrokes in an unrestricted range of harmonizing colours, which Gauguin detested. Gone were the beautiful contrasts, dear to Gauguin, the flat, thick, rough areas, reminiscent of primitive Brittany, which suited his temperament so much better. Gauguin had Spanish blood in him, and he found little he was with idealism, to him Arles spelled Babylon. He was blind in Arles, despite its climate, that compared with the tropical towns he had known. Vincent, however, was of Flemish origin, and fired as to its vulgar or prosaic features: he yielded to the brilliance and to the light which for a Dutchman is dazzling.

There were also practical issues over which they disagreed: 'First of all I was shocked by the complete and utter disorder everywhere – his box of colours was hardly big enough to hold all the squashed up tubes, none of which were ever closed, and despite all this mess, his canvas was always glowing red. The same applied to his speech, his Dutchman's brain was afire with Daudet, de Goncourt, and the Bible. The waterfront, the bridges and the boats in Arles, in fact the whole of the south, became Holland to him. He even forgot how to write in Dutch, and as can be seen from the publication of his letters to his brother, he only wrote in French...

'During the first month, I could see our finances were falling into the same state of chaos. What was I to do? It was an extremely delicate situation, as the modest funds were being supplied by his brother, who was working for Goupil – and had made a financial arrangement with me, whereby he accepted my paintings in exchange for living costs. I had to speak out and risk affronting his extreme sensitivity. I had to tackle the subject with the greatest caution and in the most persuasive manner, quite foreign to my nature. I must admit, however, that I succeeded far more easily than I expected.

'One box was now kept for outings at night, as well as for tobacco, the rent, and unforeseen expenses. On it was a piece of paper and a pencil for each of us to write honestly what we had taken from the kitty. In another box we kept the remainder of the money, divided into four parts, for weekly expenses on food. We stopped going to our little restaurant, and with the aid of a little gas stove I did the cooking, while Vincent would do the shopping, not far from the house. However there was one occasion when Vincent wanted to make a soup, but I don't know how he made his mixture – probably the same way he treats his colours on the canvas – the fact remains, we were unable to eat it. And all my good old Vincent did was to roar with laughter.'

When Gauguin was writing his memoirs, and harked back over his disagreements with Vincent, and his feelings of bitterness, let us per-

THE YELLOW CHRIST. 1889.
Albright Art Gallery, Buffalo, U.S.A.

haps call it his critical attitude, he was well aware that there were basic psychological explanations for all this, and that it arose out of the diversity of their two personalities. Nevertheless he proclaimed: 'Despite all my efforts to instill some kind of reasoned logical approach to critical views in this disorderly mind, I could never quite understand the contradictory nature of his paintings and his opinions. Thus, for example, he had unlimited admiration for Meissonier and a profound hatred for Ingres. Degas made him despair and Cézanne was no more than a humbug. To think of Monticelli made him weep.

'One of the things that made him furious was being compelled to admit I was extremely intelligent, although I had a forehead that was far too low, a sure sign of stupidity. And yet besides all this there was a tenderness, or rather an altruism that was really Christian.'

However the case may be, the two artists stimulated each other, and driven by rivalry and the urge to explain their own point of view to each other they produced a considerable amount of work. They influenced each other, though only temporarily, and came to appreciate their respective personalities. Moreover, one should realize that Gauguin was boasting when he claimed to have been playing the role of the master, and that he was exaggerating his own influence upon the development of Van Gogh, when he wrote in all seriousness:

'Without the public being aware of it, here were two men producing tremendous work, useful to both of them. And possibly to others? Certain events bear fruit. At the time I came to Arles, Vincent was full of neo-Impressionism and way out of his depth, and suffered because of it; not that this school, or any other, was particularly bad, but it simply did not suit his impatient, independent nature.

'With all these yellows over purples, all this work with complementary colours, which he went about in a disorderly fashion, he merely succeeded in producing incomplete and monotonous, subdued harmonies. The strong impact was lacking.

'I took it upon myself to enlighten him, an easy task since he was rich and fertile soil to work upon. Like all men of originality and striking personality, Vincent was never afraid of the next man and never displayed any stubbornness.

THE RED COW. 1889.
County Museum, Los Angeles.

CHRIST IN THE GARDEN OF OLIVES. 1889.
Norton Gallery and School of Fine Art, West Palm Beach, U.S.A.

'From that day on my Vincent made astonishing progress—he seemed to perceive everything that lay within him and from then on came the ever-increasing sunlight.

'Have you seen the portrait of the poet?
The face and the hair of chrome yellow 1
The attire of chrome yellow 2
The cravat of chrome yellow 3 with an emerald green pin
Against a background of chrome yellow 4.

'Without losing the slightest degree of originality, Van Gogh found in me a rich source of instruction, and every day he was grateful to me for this. This is what he means when he writes to M. Aurier that he owes a lot to Paul Gauguin.

'When I came to Arles, Vincent was trying to find himself, whereas I was much older and a mature man. I, too, am indebted to Vincent, for the knowledge that I had been useful to him reaffirmed in me the pictorial ideas I had formerly held – and also because in my more difficult moments I could recall that there existed people who were more miserable than myself.'

If one wishes to emphasize the point, it is enough to compare a few characteristic paintings by both artists, those where each has been most influenced by the other. If one places a reproduction of Van Gogh's *Walk through Arles* side by side with Gauguin's *Vision after the Sermon*, which dates from a few months before, one is struck by the similarity in the diagonal composition, with the oblique line of the yellow road in one, and the diagonal traced by the tree trunk fulfilling exactly the same purpose in the other. Moreover, Van Gogh has placed his Arlesiennes in the lefthand corner of the foreground, exactly as Gauguin did with his Breton peasant women, thus accentuating the impression of depth in the picture. This is comparable to the technique used in photography of arranging the foreground in such a way as to make it appear in relief. Finally, Van Gogh has given his women withdrawn, sulky expressions, quite unlike the good humour of southerners, however natural they may be on the austere faces of Breton women.

On the other hand, Vincent has not flattened his colour tones; as in the *Portrait of Madame Roulin and her Baby*, he treated his subjects in his own individual way, using multicoloured dots. If the over all effect of the canvas is rather more subdued than usual with Van Gogh, it is none the less lustrous for all that, displaying a vivacity that had not been present in Gauguin's canvases so far.

Gauguin painted the same subject most sensitively under the title of *Old Maids of Arles* (page 72) during the same period. He has darkened the women's capes to give them a unity and make them stand out in the cloisonnist manner. The whole landscape, constructed around the same diagonal, has been synthesised to an ex-

LITTLE GIRLS AT LE POULDU. 1889 (?)
Mme Alf. Schendle Hergiswil Collection, Unterwald, Switzerland.

treme degree, apart from the bush in the foreground, which has been etched out in short parallel brushstrokes far more broadly than usual, and yellow streaks against the mass of dark green give the sort of effect cultivated by Van Gogh. Here the influence has worked in the opposite direction.

More significant perhaps would be a comparison between the portraits of Roulin's son, Armand, by the two painters. There is the same background, the same expanse of black, making a dramatic impact in both paintings – in Van Gogh's it is the hat and the waistcoat, and with Gauguin, the hair and the drapery, probably imaginary, that hangs against the wall (page 60). But Gauguin painted Roulin's son in a black suit, thus enabling him to eliminate all details of relief, in order to define the shape the more clearly, whereas Vincent chose clothing of bright yellow, which he presented as very smooth, but brought into relief by great strokes of green, that show up the folds.

Van Gogh may have nearly always remained faithful to his bright palette, sometimes to a violent degree, but in this case it is Gauguin who appears to have allowed himself to be drawn into the use of harmonies cherished by his friend, and which appear unusual and almost strange, particularly in this painting. Moreover the colours in all the works of this period are much stronger. Would Gauguin admit the influence of Van Gogh, or would he attribute this development – which was to become more pronounced, not only in Tahiti, but in Brittany – to the warm sun and the light of Provence?

As in the argument between Gauguin and Emile Bernard as to who was the originator of synthetism, we shall ignore the rival claims. What interests us is not so much the similarities in their work, as what is individual in each of them, as well as their originality, a quality not lacking in either artist. It was exactly this, moreover, that was to precipitate the tragedy and the break between them.

THE FAMOUS EAR INCIDENT

Vincent had been driving himself hard in a protracted bout of intensive work. He had been painting sometimes in full daylight, out in the country, and sometimes at night, as in the canvases of the *Railway Café*. He had suffered from loneliness, and this is borne out by the volume of his correspondence with his brother, Theo. The expected arrival of his friend had at last given him something to look forward to with excitement. Van Gogh had been expecting to find a convalescent, but Gauguin, who was much given to exaggeration in his correspondence just to arouse sympathy, was in fact perfectly well after the spell in the invigorating air of the Breton coast.

At first it was Vincent who speeded up the pace of his life even further in a desire to show his friend everything, taking him along to meet his friends in the bistros and brothels of Arles. Then Gauguin took over, and for two months, from 20th October to 25th December, life became intense. Gauguin did not seem to notice it, but Van Gogh was overworked. He was not equal to the excessive drinking bouts and whole nights spent with the prostitutes. His state of nervous irritation grew worse and alternated with periods of exhaustion. This worried Gauguin who had been thinking of leaving, but at the thought of his going away, Van Gogh, seeing his dream of a Southern Studio vanish, became morbidly anxious in his efforts to keep him, and his attitude only served to increase Gauguin's panic reaction to get away as quickly as possible. Gauguin himself told the story in order to refute certain slanders that were levelled against him.

'I am going to reveal certain things to do with him, or rather to do with us, in order to put an end to false beliefs that have been spreading in certain circles.

'It is purely a matter of chance that in my time several men, who have sought my company and have had discussions with me, have gone mad.

'The two Van Gogh brothers are among these, and there are those with malicious intent and others who from sheer naïvety have blamed me for this madness. Obviously, some people exercise influence over others, but this is a far cry from driving them to madness.'

One wonders whether Gauguin ever felt any remorse in recalling the harsh and overbearing manner and the lack of understanding he had sometimes shown to Van Gogh. The latter had offered his friend-

SELF-PORTRAIT WITH THE YELLOW CHRIST. 1889 (?)
Private Collection.

ship with disarming naïvety, and Gauguin had never responded to this, often treating him with arrogance and condescension. However, he could feel that Vincent needed him, and hesitated to leave. The evidence for this can be found in these words which he wrote to Schuffenecker in December: 'You are awaiting me with open arms, and I thank you, but unfortunately I cannot come yet. My position here is very awkward. I owe a great deal to Van Gogh and to Vincent, and in spite of some disagreement between us, I cannot bear any ill-will to such an upright soul, who is sick, who suffers and needs me.'

THE LONELY HOUSE. 1889.
Mr and Mrs Werner E. Josten Collection, New York.

At all events, here is his version of the story:

'Towards the end of my stay, Vincent became extremely brusque and loud, and then silent. Some nights I would wake up to find Vincent standing by my bedside. Why I should have woken up then, I cannot explain.

'However I needed only to say to him in a low voice, "Vincent, what is it?", and he would go back to bed without a word, and fall into a deep sleep.

'It occurred to me to do a portrait of him as he was painting his favourite still life of the sunflowers, and when the portrait was finished, he said to me, "It's certainly me, but me gone mad".'

This took place on 22nd December.

'That same evening we went to the café. He ordered a small absinth. Suddenly he threw the glass and its contents at my head. I ducked to avoid it, and gripping him by both arms, I left the café, crossed Place Victor Hugo, and within a few minutes Vincent found himself lying on his bed, where he fell asleep and did not wake up till morning. When he awoke he was quite calm and said to me, "My dear Gauguin, I seem to remember that I insulted you last night".

'I replied, "I forgive you willingly and with all my heart, but yesterday's scene could repeat itself, and if I had hit you, I would have lost control of myself and might have strangled you. So allow me to write to your brother, and tell him I am leaving."

'My God, what a day!'

The following day, Sunday, 23rd, was even worse:

'In the evening, I had a hasty meal, and felt like going out alone, for a breath of fresh air, redolent then of laurel blossom. I had almost gone all the way across Place Victor Hugo, when I heard a familiar light step behind me, advancing quickly and jerkily. I turned round just as Vincent was rushing at me with an open razor in his hand. The look on my face must have been alarming, for he stopped short, and lowering his head, turned round and ran back in the direction of the house.

'Was I being cowardly at that moment, and should I not have disarmed him and tried to calm him down? I have often questioned my conscience, but I cannot reproach myself in any way. Let him who will criticize me.

'I went straight to a good hotel in Arles, and having asked the time, I took a room there and went up to bed.

'I was in a state of turmoil, and could not get to sleep until about three o'clock in the morning, and when I woke up it was rather late, about half-past seven.

'I went down to the square, and found a large crowd had gathered. There were policemen near our house, and a little man in a bowler hat who was the police superintendent. Here is what had happened:

'Van Gogh had returned to the house and had immediately cut his ear right away from his head. It must have taken quite a time to staunch the flow of blood, for in the morning there were a number of blood-stained towels on the floor of the two downstairs rooms. There was blood in both rooms and on the tiny staircase that led up to our bedroom. When he recovered sufficiently to go out, he wrapped his head in a beret, and went straight off to one of the brothels, where, there being no fellow-countrywoman, they found him someone he knew. He gave the man outside his ear, which had been cleaned up and sealed in an envelope, saying "Here is a souvenir of me", and then fled back to the house, went to bed, and fell asleep. He had still taken the trouble to close the shutters and put a lighted lamp on a table near to the window.

'Ten minutes later the whole of the red-light area was astir, and everyone was chattering about what had happened. I had no inkling of any of this, as I approached the door of our house, and the man in the bowler had said to me point-blank in the sternest of tones: "What have you done to your friend?" I did not know.

"Yes, you do . . . you know perfectly well . . . he's dead."

'That moment is one I would not wish on anyone, and it took me several long minutes, before I could think straight and control the violent beating of my heart. I was suffocated by the rage and indignation, and the grief and shame in all the eyes that were turned on me, and I stammered out: "Very well, Monsieur, let us go upstairs and sort this out inside." Vincent was lying curled up in bed, completely covered by the sheets he appeared to be quite lifeless. Gently, very gently, I touched the body, and from its warmth there was no doubt as to whether or not he was alive. It seemed as if I had had my sanity and all my energy restored.

'In a very low voice I said: "Monsieur, would you take great care when you wake him, and if he asks after me, tell him I have left for Paris—it might be fatal for him to see me here."

'I must admit that from that moment on this police superintendent behaved as courteously as one could wish, and acted very sensibly, sending for a doctor and a cab.

'When they woke him, Vincent asked for his friend, his pipe and his tobacco, and even thought of asking for the box that was kept downstairs and contained our money. He obviously had his doubts! However this could hardly wound me, so hardened had I already become to suffering. Vincent was taken to hospital, and no sooner had he got there than he once again became delirious.'

There would be little relevance in mentioning the rest of the story, except to acknowledge the extremes of suffering endured by this man, who gradually had his reason restored to him sufficiently to make him aware of his own condition, and make him frenziedly paint those wonderful pictures familiar to the world.

THE BLUE ROOF, OR FARM AT LE POULDU. 1890.
E. Reves Collection.

When he had recovered, Van Gogh wrote to Gauguin with great feeling on a number of occasions, as if asking for forgiveness. 'Alone in my little yellow house, as if it was perhaps my duty to remain behind, I am unhappy at the departure of my friends ... At present I reproach myself for having perhaps–I who insisted so strongly on your staying here and waiting to see how things turned out, and gave you such good reasons for doing so–I reproach myself for having perhaps been the one who compelled you to go–unless you had planned to leave anyway? And in that case it was perhaps up to me to show that I still had a right to be kept informed.

'At all events, we still like each other sufficiently, I hope, to be able to start up once again together, if hard times, which alas are always with us impoverished artists, necessitated such a step.

'... Ah! my dear friend, for us painting is like the music of Berlioz and Wagner ... a consolation for heavy hearts! There are only a few of us, like you and me, who feel this.

'My brother understands you very well, and when he tells me that you are an unhappy type like me, then that proves how well he understands us ... I shall send you your things ...' And a postscript says: 'I would be so glad if you would write to me again.'

No doubt Gauguin was hurt when he learned that Theo compared him to Vincent, for he did not feel the least bit psychologically unbalanced, and in fact his megalomania, his obsession for travel, and his impulses to run away were all no more than somewhat extreme traits in a perfectly normal man. Thus he wrote in his Memoirs:

'Long after the catastrophe, Vincent wrote to me from the mental hospital, where he was receiving treatment. He said: "How lucky you are to be in Paris. It is still the place to find the leading figures, and you should certainly consult a specialist to cure you of your madness–shouldn't we all?" It was good advice, which is why I did not follow it, no doubt from sheer perversity.'

It was in Le Pouldu that Gauguin learned that Van Gogh had committed suicide on 27th July 1890 by shooting himself, after he

ENTRANCE TO THE FARM. 1890.
Mme L. Matthiesen Collection, Stockholm.

CARIBBEAN WOMAN. 1889 (?)
Dr and Mrs Harry Bakwin Collection, New York.

had gone off to paint as usual on the Auvers plateau. Certain biographers have reproached Gauguin for the apparent indifference he
displayed in a letter to Emile Bernard:

'I have heard the news of Vincent's death, and I am glad that you
were at the funeral. Sad as his death may be, it does not distress me
unduly, for I foresaw it and I knew what suffering the poor fellow
endured in his struggle against his madness. To have died at this time
is a great relief for him, it has put an end to his suffering, and if he

passes on to another life, he will reap the reward for his good conduct in this world (according to the Buddhist doctrine). He had the consolation of not having been abandoned by his brother, and of being understood by a few artists . . .'

These words were a tribute to his unfortunate friend, a tribute which he was to repeat in *Avant et Après,* where he himself acknowledged with great discretion the fond affection he cherished in his heart for poor Vincent.

'The last letter I received was headed Auvers, near Pontoise. He told me that he had hoped to be sufficiently cured to come and join me in Brittany, but that he had been compelled to recognize the impossibility of any cure.

' "Dear Master" (the only time he uttered this word) "it is more dignified, after having known you and caused you distress, to die in full possession of my mind, than in a condition that would be a degradation to you."

'And he shot himself in the stomach, and it was not until several hours later, lying on his bed, smoking his pipe, and with his mind perfectly clear that he died, with love for his art and bearing others no hatred.'

In *The Monsters,* Jean Dolent writes: 'When Gauguin says, "Vincent" his voice is gentle.' Guessing, rather than knowing, Jean Dolent spoke the truth.

THE UNIVERSAL EXHIBITION OF 1889

Back in Paris, Gauguin moved temporarily into a small studio on the Avenue Montsouris, and as he was now dreaming of travelling, all his time was taken up with active participation in several shows. If he sold enough, he could set off on his travels again . . . to Martinique, Madagascar, or elsewhere. He eagerly awaited the opening of the Universal Exhibition, which he visited, dreaming of distant horizons. He had sent eleven canvases to the Exhibition of the Twenty, being held in Brussels. He had raised his prices, and these now ranged between 500 and 1,000 francs. But the Belgian public

IA ORANA MARIA. 1891.
Metropolitan Museum of Art, New York.

was as unresponsive as the French public, and not a single buyer came forward.

In Paris Theo van Gogh was doing his best to make him known, but patrons of art were rare, especially since there had been a further deterioration in the financial crisis – the Panama Canal Company had gone into liquidation, and the director of the Discount Bank had committed suicide.

Nevertheless on the Champ de Mars preparations were going forward for the Exhibition; the Eiffel Tower was nearing completion, and a Palace of Fine Arts reserved for Cormon, Meissonier and Jérôme was being built. The only Impressionists represented were Monet and Pissarro. But the hard-working Schuffenecker organized an exhibition of the works of his friends in the Café Volpini, on the ground floor of this same Palace. At the outset Gauguin wanted to restrict it exclusively to their friends: 'Remember that this is not to be an exhibition *for the others* ... Remember that we are the ones who are doing the inviting, consequently ... Schuff – ten canvases, Guillaumin – ten, Gauguin – ten, Bernard – ten, Roy – two, man from Nancy – two, Vincent – six ... That should be quite enough. For my part, I refuse to exhibit with the *others*, Pissarro, Seurat, etc.,' he wrote to Schuffenecker from Pont-Aven, where he had once again retreated. When he returned to Paris in April he encountered widespread disagreement. Theo did not wish to lend Vincent's pictures – 'the back stairs are no way to make an entrance!' – Guillaumin was undecided ... Laval, Anquetin, Georges-Daniel de Monfreid and Léon Fauché (the 'man from Nancy') were to complete the group.

A vast crowd was to come to the Champ de Mars and to visit the Café Volpini. Sérusier was won over and declared, 'I'm on your side!' The young critic Albert Aurier became a friend of the 'Impressionist and Synthetist Group' to whom he opened up the columns of the avant-garde periodical, *Le Moderniste*, of which he was chief editor. In it Gauguin published 'Notes on art at the Universal Exhibition'. He expressed his disgust for everything and everyone; he was becoming embittered. He paid lengthy visits to the foreign pavilions, and admired the exhibits from India and the West Indies. His

122

desire to travel was stronger than ever, but he returned temporarily to Brittany in June.

But Pont-Aven was transformed; chaos reigned. Gauguin promptly left with Sérusier for Le Pouldu, where they moved into the extremely humble Hotel Destais. 'I am in a fisherman's inn right on the sea shore, near a village of five hundred inhabitants, I live like a peasant and am considered unsociable ... I spend one franc a day on food and two sous on tobacco. I talk to no one. I have an exhibition of my works—alone—at Goupil's in Paris, and they are causing quite a stir, but they are very difficult to sell ...'

LE POULDU — THE SPIRIT OF BRITTANY

Artist friends had come to join him, including Charles Laval, and Meyer de Haan, a slightly hump-backed Dutchman—he and Gauguin made a strange sight walking along together; then there were Filiger, Maufra, Sérusier and Moret. Gauguin spent a lot of time looking at the countryside and reflecting, but he did very little painting. Then during August, as he had no more money, he left Le Pouldu and returned to Pont-Aven, where he could always be sure of obtaining credit, and within the space of a few weeks he produced most of the masterpieces of his Breton period, *Calvary*, *The Yellow Christ* and *La Belle Angèle*, among others. The inspiration for these came from the *Pietà* at Nizon, which he had come across in the sand dunes near Le Pouldu, and the cross of the little chapel of Tremalo, and lastly, the daughter of the proprietors of the little bistro close to the Pension Gloanec, who was married to a man named Frédéric Sâtre.

In these compositions Gauguin was entirely free in his treatment of reality—he not only 'synthesised', he 'symbolised'. There is a density in these works that makes them reminiscent of icons, but they differ from them in their critical attitude. Gauguin was attracted by the primitive almost barbaric quality of Breton mysticism, while at the same time seeming to mock at its fervour. It moved him; he would have liked to be religious, but he knew religion too well to be able to subscribe to it wholeheartedly. What he needed were the simple

REVERIE. 1891.
William Rockhill Nilson Collection, Gallery of Art, Kansas City, U.S.A.

cults of the South Sea Islands, but he might have been suspected of only vaguely understanding them and giving them an individual interpretation of his own.

The painting of the *Calvary* as well as *The Yellow Christ* can be divided into three basic elements, as integrally related to each other as the movements of a symphony. There is the cross itself, terrifying as a totem, and mysterious as a pre-Columbian statue, with its greenish mass rising up, barely recognizable as the granite from which it was actually carved – a symbol of an incomprehensible faith. Behind the desolate world of the sand dunes covered with sparse grass stretches out in yellow, orange and pale green waves a desert in which the blue line of the Atlantic seems more alive than the poor, bent figures that appear here and there. In the foreground, in front of the cross, there is a powerful, ageless peasant woman in a pose that recalls the lines of the cross, with a sheep, symbolizing life and human beliefs; the woman is not praying, but looks rather as if she were standing there to shelter from the wind. A powerfully moving impression of loneliness and forlornness emerges from this composition with its remarkably unity.

Even more dramatic still is *The Yellow Christ* (page 104), painted in sweeping strokes, gaunt, highly stylized, with elongated outstretched arms, and almost lifelike in its colouring – one has the uncomfortable sensation of being face to face with a real corpse, that is human rather than divine. Three women in Breton costume kneel at his feet in attitudes of contemplation, bordering on indifference, resigned to the inevitability of fate. The long line of Christ's elongated body, and the cross stretching right across the top of the canvas, are in harsh contrast to the soft curves of the landscape in harmonies of yellow, green and red, and the musical rhythm of the arabesques. What Gauguin appears to be conveying is all the suffering endured by man alone in the sweetness of the world.

This was indeed his message. His *Christ in the Garden of Olives* (page 107), which is virtually a self-portrait, pursues the same theme. In his *Self-Portrait with the Yellow Christ* (page 112), he has bowed the head of Christ to the right and not to the left, in order to cor-

125

respond with the position of his own face, a large face in semi-profile, well-defined in relief, but with inscrutable features, not sorrowful but sad, the eyes looking obliquely beyond, towards a future without hope.

There is a whole history behind the portrait of *La Belle Angèle* (page 77). It was generally agreed that she was the prettiest girl in Pont-Aven. As a way of thanking her parents for the credit they let him have, Gauguin thought he would paint her portrait. He placed her in a circular inset in the lower righthand part of the picture, and covered the rest of the canvas with floral symbols and a strange Peruvian-looking statuette. A fertility goddess? It is unimportant. The fact remains that this sumptuous and original composition had a frigid reception, and the gift was rejected in horror. The husband, no Apollo himself, fancied he saw a caricature of himself in the pre-Columbian statuette. By exaggerating the thinness of her lips, the narrow slyness of her eyes, and the prominence of her cheek-bones, Gauguin's treatment had been so 'synthetist', that the portrait looked like a caricature.

It makes an interesting story to hear what the sitter later had to say on the subject to Charles Chassé, when he was endeavouring to gather first-hand information about the Pont-Aven school:

'Gauguin was a very gentle person and very unhappy, and we were quite fond of him. Only at that time his way of painting seemed rather alarming. He was always telling my husband he would like to paint my portrait, and then one day he actually began it. But while he was working on it he never wanted to let me see the canvas, because he said you couldn't get any idea of what it would look like before it was finished; and so he would always cover it up after each sitting. When he had finished, he showed it first of all to the other painters and they made fun of it a good deal, and I got to know about this. So that when he came to bring it to me, I was already prejudiced against it; my mother had told me: "It seems that the artists had a fight over your picture last night. What a lot of fuss they're making because of you!" Gauguin arrived, very pleased with himself, and went through the house trying to find the best place to hang it. But when he showed it to me, I said: "How awful!", and told him he could take it straight back with him, and that I never wanted anything like that in my house. Imagine! All that time ago, and in a tiny little place like this! Especially since I knew practically nothing about painting then! Gauguin was very sad, and disappointed, and said it was the most successful portrait he had ever painted. Naturally, after that we became rather cool towards him, and I hardly ever saw him. Since then I heard that at the Degas sale, my portrait, which I refused as a present, fetched several tens of thousands of francs.'

Bearing in mind the prestige Gauguin had meanwhile acquired, and the commercial value the painting now had, it is more than likely that this account of the facts had been considerably toned down, and one can imagine the gross and brutal way in which Gauguin's present was turned down. It made him suffer all the more, since it was the second time this had happened to him.

Two years earlier, full of satisfaction at the way his *Vision after the Sermon* had turned out, he had set off on foot for Nizon to see the priest, and had offered him his masterpiece as a gift to decorate the little church. The priest was horrified, wondering whether to interpret this suggestion as a provocation and a sacrilege or whether to regard it as a dauber's idea of a joke. Having endured words that were cruelly wounding to his pride, for all the ecclesiastical unction in which they were couched, Gauguin turned round and went back along the road to Pont-Aven, his painting still under his arm.

As may be gathered from Angèle Sâtre's allusion to the fights the painters had over her portrait, Gauguin's works were regarded as controversial in the narrow circle of artists at Pont-Aven, some defending him hotly, others criticizing him even more violently.

It is difficult to imagine the sort of atmosphere that must have prevailed in these poor country inns, invaded by groups of artists. There are many descriptions, but the essential character of the life is difficult to reconstruct. Thus, in a letter to Charles Chasse, M. Motheré described in detail the main room of the inn at Le Pouldu, to which Gauguin had returned in September 1889. This time they did not go

HEAD OF A TAHITIAN GIRL. 1891–93.
Private Collection.

to the Hotel Destais but moved into the wine shop on the beach, kept by Marie Henry, known as Marie Poupée, who was quite openly bestowing her favours on his friend, Meyer de Haan, without caring what people said. The artists had virtually taken over the dining-room, and completely filled it with their works. On the ceiling, around a scene depicting a goose picking fleas out of a woman's hair, were the words: 'Honi soit qui mal y pense' (Evil to him who evil thinks). A still life with onions bore the inscription: 'I love

HEAD OF A TAHITIAN MAN. 1891–93.

onions fried in oil'. Another still life in the style of Seurat, was traditionally greeted with jokes about '*Monsieur Ripipoint*' ('dot-and-carry-one'). On another wall was Wagner's creed: 'I believe in a Last Judgment where all those who in this world have dared to trade in sublime and chaste art, all those who have sullied and degraded it by the baseness of their sentiments and their covetous desire for material possessions, will be damned to purgatory.' Finally, on the door to the bar hung *Bonjour Monsieur Gauguin* (page 93).

Gauguin did another very similar version of this painting, and in both we see him dressed in the attire that was to make him so conspicuous during the following winter in Paris. The second painting (page 89) is seen from a closer viewpoint, and the figures are comparatively larger. Here Gauguin's face is pallid beneath an enormous navy blue beret, as he stands before the peasant woman who is opening the gate for him. He is hidden in a kind of washed-out Inverness cape ranging in colour from rust to verdigris. He is a sort of mysterious messenger, of undistinguished appearance, but his paleness and rigid bearing lend him the power of irresistible fascination. Indeed, he really did look like one of the Magi or some chieftain during those last two seasons of his comings and goings between Pont-Aven and Le Pouldu.

He did an enormous amount of work there, turning out scenes with figures, peasant women dancing, harvesting, watching flocks of sheep. Several of the young girls he painted already have that distant, 'inward-turned' look that was to reappear on his Tahitian women.

Gauguin also enjoyed doing caricatures, like the one he did of his friend, Meyer de Haan, emphasizing his deformity. He himself appeared with a halo round his head, holding a snake in his hand, his face enigmatically locked between the deep red of the background and the yellow mass of the clothing (page 92). A real Inca head! No doubt he was already dreaming of the Peru of his childhood, and of the lands awaiting him.

But painting alone did not satisfy him, and he had a heavy basketful of limewood sent to him, carving extraordinary figures from it with his chisel – once again anticipating his future development. He described this in a letter to Emile Bernard: '. . . I have done something better and even more strange. Gauguin (as a monster) grasping the hand of a protesting woman, and saying to her: "Be amorous and you will be happy" (Soyez amoureuses, vous serez heureuses) (page 96). The fox, the Indian symbol of perversity, and then in the interstices small figures. The wood will be coloured.' Indeed, the work is disturbingly exotic and he was to repeat this success with its partner, *Be mysterious* (Soyez mystérieuses).

The speed with which as a matter of principle he worked amazed those who watched him. It is better to start a picture all over again than to attempt to correct it, he maintained, and he would aim at 'dashing off a picture' in one go. He always looked around him for a long while and knew his subject 'by heart' before starting to paint. He would begin by constructing his picture with strong blue or purple lines, marking out the composition and outlining the details of certain shapes. Then the work of painting itself would begin – one might be led to believe that all there was for him to do was to fill in the areas he had outlined in his initial drawing. But he did more. Each part was covered in tiny strokes, closely placed, parallel, upright or more often oblique strokes until the whole surface had acquired a perfect density. The colour was never uniform: yellows went over into orange, browns burst into red, greens varied and were paler in places, and the whites were never white, nor even alike – they were grey and discoloured. Thus each part of the picture was entirely homogeneous, without being either monochrome or monotonous. In the end the contrasting areas would complement each other and create a rhythmical harmony.

NEITHER FAME NOR FORTUNE

As the winter advanced Gauguin became dispirited. No prospect of a sale! He had turned down a sale to the writer Félicien Champsaur, who had offered him an absurd sum. A countess had promised to secure him State commissions, which never came to anything. He painted less, was always declaiming, encouraged in this by the presence of Sérusier who loved to theorize, and a new disciple, Filiger. He wrote letters to his friends in which he gave vent to his grievances, and tried to ease the bitterness in his heart. '... all this mounting bile and gall brought on me by the redoubled blows of misfortune is making me ill, and at the moment I have barely the strength or the inclination to work. And at one time work used to make me forget ... In the end I shall pass on, after all what is man in this immense creation, and who am I more than any other to complain?'

To this, he gave his own reply: 'An impressionist artist, that is to say a rebel.' He certainly had good reason to complain! '. . . I am making a few studies, quite mechanically . . . but my heart is not in it . . . I see my family abandoned, deprived of parental support, and not a soul to whom I can unburden my suffering . . .'

Here are some details that might give the artists of today food for thought: 'Since January [the letter was written in November] I have received nine hundred and twenty-five francs from sales, and at the age of forty-two to have to live on that and buy colours, etc. . . . is enough to daunt the most hardened person.'

The news he had from Paris, and the reactions to the pictures he was regularly sending Theo van Gogh, did not help to sustain his morale, but he felt that he had found a truth, and he had no intention of giving way in the realm of art. '. . . I am ready to declare myself beaten by events, by men, and by my family, but not by public opinion. This does not interest me, and I am quite prepared to do without admirers.' He became increasingly preoccupied with the desire to find solitude and happiness in another land. He was now to return to Paris, and try to carry out his plans for emigration.

Thanks to Schuffenecker, who paid his fare early in February, he was able to make his way to his friend's home, which was now in the Plaisance district, at 12 rue Alfred-Durand-Claye. He behaved abominably towards him, being sour and bitter, and taking over his friend's studio as if it were his rightful due. There was no limit to the ingratitude with which he responded to Schuffenecker's loyalty; it was even said that he took advantage of the disorder he had caused in the Schuffenecker home to seduce his wife.

All his efforts to find some money proved fruitless, and he returned to Pont-Aven during May 1890. From then on Gauguin thought of nothing but arranging his escape to a better civilization.

THE LAST SEASON IN BRITTANY

In the spring of 1890 at Le Pouldu there began a new period in Gauguin's life. He engaged in endless aesthetic discussions of pictorial

TAHITIAN NUDES AND A DOG. 1892 (?).
Honolulu Academy of Arts, Hawaï.

symbolism with his friends and a new follower, the artist, Filiger, but meanwhile his mind was elsewhere. He did very little painting, and there were no new developments in his style. He continued in the same brilliant vein as in the previous summer, with scenes of Breton peasant women and little girls with low foreheads.

Gauguin was dreaming of the future but he also took certain practical steps. What had previously been no more than a vague longing now became a firm intention. He was determined to achieve a triple objective – to obtain the necessary practical information (he asked Emile Bernard several times to enquire after departure dates of boats, and about the cost of passages), secondly, to persuade one of his friends to accompany him, and finally to find the funds.

His letters now became manifestos in favour of the various countries that he contemplated settling in. His efforts at persuasion were concentrated on Emile Bernard, Schuffenecker and Meyer de Haan. He painted the life awaiting them there in idyllic colours: a huge hut that would serve as a studio, where they could keep house for themselves; according to an oft-repeated phrase, their living expenses would be 'nil'. There would be no difficulty in find-ing models there – they would be there for the asking, since the women went about the countryside naked! He supported his own arguments with the accounts of travellers whom he had questioned on their way through Brittany. He even went so far as to recom-mend the tender and affectionate natures of the native women, who, in this respect, he maintained were superior to European women.

In order to reach this paradise, he had to raise enough money for the fare. If need be, he was prepared to take a single ticket! Ever optimistic, he was quite confident that he would manage once he was there. He entertained various hopes in turn. 'Charlopin', a doctor and inventor, was expecting to receive a fabulous sum for the sale of the patent on one of his inventions and offered to buy a batch of canvases from Gauguin for a round sum of 5,000 francs, once he received the fortune he was counting on. Gauguin unhesitat-ingly accepted this unusual offer. The deal was not a wonderful com-mercial proposition, but it would enable him to rid himself of his debts and to leave. Unfortunately the project seemed to be indefinitely delayed . . .

Schuffenecker had just sold the small rolled-gold business which he had built up with a friend, and had made a substantial profit. Gauguin took a chance, approached him and eloquently presented his travelling plans as a perfectly sound and worthwhile venture. But despite the accusations that Gauguin was to level at him, it was not so much timidity as prudence, and his sound knowledge of his friend over many years, that prompted Schuffenecker politely to decline. He was bent on having some flats built in order to give his children security for the future. Such a typically bourgeois form of investment infuriated Gauguin, and a total break between them was only narrowly avoided. Several months later Gauguin learned that his friend was now about to sell a piece of land that he had held for a long time, and once again he summoned all his charm and persuasiveness, but in vain. Schuffenecker would not hear of it.

Meyer de Haan was physically disabled, which discouraged him from taking part in an adventure such as this. He lived quite comfortably on a small private income. Was it for this reason, or out of a genuine liking for his friend and a wish to shake him out of the drab existence that he led, that Gauguin sought to take him with him in search of brighter shores? For a moment Meyer de Haan weakened, but his attachment to the Breton landscape made him change his mind, for it was this that inspired him to paint his peaceful landscapes in a discreetly cloisonnist style. But Gauguin did not lose heart and meanwhile his plans for his journey changed.

For a while he had hopes of getting a post in Tonkin, and approached several ministers to this end, encouraging Schuffenecker to do likewise. They would benefit from the special privileges accorded to those who went as settlers to France's newest territories. Admiral Courbet's final conquest of Tonkin was only made in 1883, and the treaty signed as recently as 1885. But the Tonkinese project fell through.

Gauguin's thoughts now fixed on Madagascar. He had first heard about it from the wife of the painter Odilon Redon, who was a

TE TIARE FARANI — THE FLOWERS OF FRANCE. 1891.
Hermitage Museum, Leningrad.

native of the island. France only possessed certain 'institutions' on the main island, dating back to the seventeenth century. It is just as well that Gauguin did not go there, for in 1895 there were troubles followed by a bloody expedition, which handed the protectorate over to Queen Ranavalo...

Allowing his imagination free rein, Gauguin built up a marvellous and romantic future for himself. 'On five thousand francs you can live for thirty years... You can get your food quite simply by hunting.' 'Ask Bernard to get me text-books on Malagasy, it must be possible to find this in Paris.'

'What I want to do is to set up a Studio of the Tropics. With the money I shall have, I shall be able to buy a native hut, like the ones you saw at the Universal Exhibition, made of wood and mud, and covered with thatch, close to the town, but in the countryside. This costs next to nothing, I shall build on to it by cutting down wood, and make it into a comfortable home. We will have a cow, hens and fruit trees, all the main ingredients of our diet, and in the end it will cost us nothing to live. Free...'

Gauguin was obsessed by this illusion of liberty, and it was this that drove him to leave. His pride suffered cruelly from the approaches he was compelled to make to dealers simply in order to exist, and from the blunt judgments they would make about his work. To live for nothing meant escaping the humiliations he had to endure in Europe. It also meant freedom to paint as he liked without having to make any compromises. There was an element of eroticism in his plans. Since he had left Denmark, he had been leading an austere life. He envisaged the tropics as a place where there was complete sexual freedom, a paradise on earth: 'Over there women are for the asking, which will provide me with a model every day. And I promise you that the Madagascan woman has a heart just as much as the Frenchwoman, except that she is far less calculating!' In everything he displayed an optimism that bordered on naïvety. Finally he says: 'Exactly half my daily bread I shall put at your disposal.' But Emile Bernard did not go.

Despite his own hesitations, Bernard nevertheless had a decisive influence on Gauguin. It was he who first suggested: 'Why not Tahiti?' Had Gauguin read *Le mariage de Loti*, which had been published about ten years ago? At first Gauguin rejected the idea but it was gradually to take a hold. The women of Madagascar, he maintained, are 'just as sweet in Tahiti', besides, many of them came of Polynesian stock. He compared the mortality rates of the two places, and cast doubts on the reliability of Loti's view of the island, for he had seen it through the eyes of a well-to-do writer. 'I must admit,' he wrote in June 1890, 'that Tahiti certainly has its advantages.' He was to set sail less than a year later.

MADEMOISELLE VAÏTÉ GOUPIL. C. 1891.
Private Collection.

He was already deploring the fact that 'one must allow three months for the journey ... Find out how much it would cost ...' 'I now only live for this hope of the promised land ... The future is rather dark for our children, even with a few pence in this rotten and corrupt Europe ... The Tahitians, on the other hand, the happy inhabitants of the unknown paradise of the South Sea Islands, know only the sweetness of life. For them living means singing and loving.' He was so obsessed by the thought of the lands that awaited him

PORTRAIT OF MISS CAMBRIDGE. 1891.
Brussels Museum.

and the life that was to be his, that he admitted: 'With this great journey ahead of me I am no longer working.' He urged his friends: 'Write to me often and do not leave anything undone as far as our departure is concerned, or rather our liberty.' This was not strong enough. 'I shall come to Paris and move heaven and earth.' But his friends did not have the same compelling reasons for leaving. 'I need to come to Paris in order to sort things out, and I owe more than three hundred francs at the hotel ...'

A sudden source of hope came with a telegram from Theo van Gogh. 'Departure for Tropics assured. Money follows', then, 'Send all your output. Have certain sale'. Gauguin did not dare to believe it. He was quite right. The money never arrived. Theo in turn had gone mad.

Theo had been deeply affected by the death of his brother in the previous summer, and had given up his post at Boussod-Valadon's to start up an artists' association. He sent these two misleading telegrams while he was in a state of delirium, and attempted to kill his young wife and baby son. He was confined to Dr Blanche's clinic, where he died the following year.

This was a bitter disappointment for Gauguin, who did not yet know how great a loss it was for him, and was feeling sorry only for himself. But a chance stroke of luck was to deliver him once again. Thanks to Emile Bernard, he sold five canvases at 100 francs apiece to a Luxembourg collector, Eugène Boch, and without wasting any further time, he returned to Paris to arrange his departure.

As in the previous winter he made his way to the Place de l'Odéon and in the Café Voltaire met the symbolist poets and writers, whose activities were to help him make himself known. There was some reservation about the application of symbolist theories to painting, but he accepted as only natural the friendly goodwill that was spontaneously extended to him. For his friends he was to be *the* great symbolist painter.

The group would meet on Monday evenings after dinner. Verlaine could be seen there, already aged and sick, and there were other poets, Jean Moréas, and Charles Morice, who was regarded as the leader of the young school. There was also Albert Aurier, the critic, who had already written about Gauguin's work on a number of occasions and who had gained an impressive reputation with his column in the *Mercure de France*, the new symbolist review. Carrière, the sculptor came fairly regularly, and Rodin put in an occasional appearance.

AREAREA — PRANKS. 1892.
Louvre, Paris.

Despite his sad expression, his unconventional attire and his poverty, Gauguin made a number of acquaintances. Aurier introduced him to Alfred Vallette, the director of the *Mercure,* and his wife, the novelist, Rachilde, and to other poets – Henri de Régnier, Stuart Merril, Jean Dolent, and Stéphane Mallarmé, who invited him to his famous 'Tuesdays'.

As far as the Ecole des Beaux-Arts and the Academies were concerned, Sérusier and his friends, the Nabis, had campaigned widely for Gauguin, whom they proclaimed as their master. Maurice Denis had published several studies of him and raised Gauguin's teaching to the status of a theory. The only ones to criticize him severely were Emile Bernard, who had just had a fit of conscience, and Pissarro, possibly jealous of the fame of his former pupil. For the old Impressionist, Gauguin's painting was an affectation. For Bernard, it was no more than an imitation of his own discoveries. Gauguin, regarded as an eccentric and a lone-wolf, now led a thoroughly Parisian life and got himself talked about.

He also often visited Georges–Daniel de Monfreid whom he had met on his return from Martinique. Monfreid painted under the pseudonym of Georges Daniel. It was memories of the sea and the sailor's life that drew these two men together, since Monfreid had in fact owned a boat and had sailed from the Atlantic to the Mediterranean. He was nicknamed 'Captain'.

He also often visited Georges-Daniel de Monfreid whom he had strained, since the latter had come down on the side of Emile Bernard, Daniel de Monfreid lent him his studio. Monfreid had a mistress who worked as a seamstress. When they left the studio, Gauguin would accompany his friend, and he in turn struck up an idyllic relationship with a seamstress by the name of Juliette Huet. By the time Gauguin left France, she was expecting a baby.

In 1949 Pierre Descargues went on behalf of the paper *Arts* to interview Gauguin's daughter, who was an artist using the name of Germaine Chardaine, and was surprised to hear her utter the words 'my father' without the slightest trace of bitterness. Her mother, on the other hand, who was then eighty-three years old (she died in 1955), maintained a stubborn silence. When Gauguin died, she had sold the pictures she had been given for an absurdly low price, and thrown out all the souvenirs of the man who had been her lover for a few months, and whom she had refused to follow to Tahiti. This was Gauguin's first adventure of this kind.

In his letters to his wife, Gauguin had always been declaring his fidelity to her, and complained that he was getting small reward for it. With the advent of Juliette Huet yet another tie between him and his wife was broken, and he had taken one more step in the direction of this absolute freedom that was to mean happiness for him.

Unfortunately the selling of works of art was going through a bad period, particularly the kind of works he had to offer. Maurice Joyant had taken the place of Theo van Gogh at Boussod-Valadon's; he liked Gauguin's painting very much, but could not make his clients share his enthusiasm. Charles Morice was unsuccessful in his attempts to interest personalities like Georges Clémenceau or the former minister of Fine Arts, Antonin Proust. He then suggested to Gauguin that there should be a grand sale of his works.

This was arranged with a great deal of care, and supported by a campaign in the press. Mallarmé recommended Gauguin to Octave Mirbeau, the novelist and pamphleteer, who was to make a name for himself with his realist novels, like *Le Journal d'une femme de chambre* (Diary of a Chamber-Maid) and his famous comedy, *Les Affaires sont les affaires* (Business is Business).

On 16th February Octave Mirbeau published the introduction he had written to the catalogue, in the *Echo de Paris*, and in the *Figaro* of the 18th he wrote a feature on the artist. With his natural enthusiasm and his volatile temperament he emphasized the originality of Gauguin's approach.

'I gather that Monsieur P. Gauguin is about to leave for Tahiti. He intends to live there alone for several years, to build his hut, and work afresh on those ideas that have obsessed him. I am intrigued and moved by this case of a man, fleeing from civilization, in voluntary pursuit of silence and forgetfulness, the better to become aware of himself, the better to give ear to those inner voices that are drowned in the roar of our passions and disputes. Paul Gauguin is a quite exceptional, and most disturbing artist, who rarely appears in public, and whom consequently the public hardly knows. I have often intended writing about him. But unfortunately one is always so short of time, why I cannot say. Possibly it was because I shrank from the difficulty of such a task, and the fear of speaking inadequately of a man for whom I have a high and very special regard. To pinpoint in a few brief and rapid notes the significance of Gauguin's art, which is so complicated and yet so primitive, so clear and so obscure, so barbaric and so sophisticated, is surely impossible, or

TWO WOMEN ON THE BEACH. 1891.
Louvre, Paris.

should I say outside my own capabilities? To do justice to such a
man and such work as he has produced would take a study of far
greater length than can be accommodated in the meagre space allowed
by any journal. However, I believe that by pointing out, first of all
Gauguin's intellectual leanings, and by referring briefly to some of
the characteristic features of his strange and tormented life, the work
itself becomes clearer and illuminated with a brighter light.'

And Mirbeau ended: '... the same dream never remains for long
in this racing mind of his, it grows until it becomes clearer, and then
it is once more the nostalgia of his earliest memories of distant lands.

PARAU PARAU – WORDS, WORDS (OR GOSSIP). 1891.
Hermitage Museum, Leningrad.

... The same need for silence, for meditation, and absolute solitude which drove him to Martinique, now drives him even farther afield, to Tahiti, where nature is more congenial to his dreams, where he hopes the tender caresses of the Pacific Ocean will restore him to an old and safe ancestral love. Wherever he goes, Monsieur Paul Gauguin may be assured that our affectionate devotion will accompany him.'

Gauguin now lived through hours of intense and feverish excitement, but he was confident; he wrote letter upon letter to his wife, feeling sure his victory was imminent: 'There will surely come a day when *your children* may present themselves before anyone anywhere, with their father's name to assure them protection and respect.'

On article after another appeared in the press. On Friday 20th February there was Roger-Marx in *Le Voltaire*, and on Sunday, the day before the sale, Gustave Geffroy in *Le Gaulois* and *La Justice*.

FIRST RECOGNITION

The sale was held on 23rd February and was, comparatively speaking, a success, a prestige success maybe, but a success nevertheless. Gauguin sold twenty-nine of the thirty canvases for close on 10,000 francs of the period, equivalent to approximately £2,000 today.

A large public attended, composed of connoisseurs, art dealers, patrons of the arts, collectors and artists, and those whose curiosity had been aroused by the articles in the press. The chief attraction of the sale was the auction of the *Vision after the Sermon*, which had been rejected by the priest of Nizon, and which went to the collector, Henry Meilheurat des Pruraux for the sum of 900 francs. Degas bought *La Belle Angèle* for 450 francs. Méry Laurent, Mallarmé's friend, bought a Breton landscape, and Daniel de Monfreid a canvas of Martinique. Not a single work fetched less than 250 francs.'

The Hotel Drouot that day was also the scene of the final break between Emile Bernard and Gauguin. Madeleine Bernard, who had accompanied her brother, publicly accused Gauguin of having deprived Bernard of his rightful position as discoverer of synthetism. Gauguin ignored the incident, and his friends backed him up.

We have a description of Gauguin on the eve of his departure by Jean de Rotonchamp, alias Brouillon, a friend of Gauguin, and author of the first serious monograph of the artist, which was published in Weimar in 1906 and appeared in Paris under the imprint of Crès in 1925. 'His voice was low and rough, which may have been the effect of arthritis, or the result of too much tobacco smoking, for Gauguin would never be without a cigarette, except when he was smoking a clay pipe.

'His hair had begun to lose its original colour, and was now taking on an indeterminate shade. Originally it had been chestnut-coloured

146

bordering on red, but now it had lost its colour. Under this thick and curling mass of hair, his forehead was broad and somewhat low. His heavy-lidded eyes were greenish-grey. The nose was strong and hooked. His moustache was thin and lighter than the colour of his hair, revealing a full mouth, with slightly down-turned corners. Beneath this broad mouth, was a receding chin, covered with a curly, but short, thin beard.

'Without going into any ethnographic details, there is no doubt that Gauguin's head, though not typical of any one specific southern race, was nevertheless certainly not that of a European of the northern climate. The grandson of Chazal and Flora Tristan was in looks as well as in fact of mixed blood.'

Thus when he went to say farewell to his children, who had not seen him for six years, they did not recognize him!

FAREWELL TO THE FAMILY

There only remained for him to embrace his children for the last time. He was never to see them again. He had been longing to come and visit them for a long time, but his wife had discouraged him from doing so. The day before the sale, he wrote to Mette: 'If it is a success, ... may I come to Copenhagen to embrace my children, without you and your family accusing me of being *irresponsible*? Don't worry, I shall not be any trouble to you, I shall stay at a hotel for the few days I shall spend incognito in Copenhagen.'

He arrived on 7th March. The children had grown – Emile, the eldest, was nearly seventeen years old, Aline was fourteen, Clovis twelve, Jean-René ten, and little Pola, seven. His wife met him at the station with the two eldest children, Emile and Aline. Pola, who retained some family memories, has given us an account of this meeting. They were surprised by Gauguin's long hair and the way in which he had put on weight; he was surprised at Mette's short hair, and how badly his children spoke French. A joke was enough to break the ice, and they avoided the issues that affected them most deeply, and spoke of practical questions. Mette remained resolutely

NAFEA FOA IPOIPO – WHEN WILL YOU BE MARRIED? 1892.
Kunstmuseum, Basle.

aloof. She did not wish to be hurt by allowing herself to succumb to renewed affection; 'she found him so changed that her anguish at the thought of living together once again got the better of her desire to be affectionate to him, for she pitied him just as much as she pitied herself,' writes Pola, this being the official opinion of the Gad family! 'She clung to the present, whereas he was thinking of the future.'

Gauguin was profoundly disturbed by this encounter with what for him was already the past. By her tangible presence, Mette suddenly once again became his wife, but as often happens when separated couples meet, the children came between them and acted as a barrier. Gauguin was to keep the memory of the drives in a landau, accompanied by Emile in his college uniform, and Aline, whose affection consoled him for the understandable coolness of his wife. He returned to Paris after a short while, and the tone of his letters changed – admittedly only temporarily. 'My dear Mette' became 'My adored Mette', 'an adoration that is often touched with bitterness ... when we are white-haired, we can, in place of passion, enter a period of peace and spiritual happiness, surrounded by our children ...'

At seven o'clock on 23rd March, Gauguin's friends held a farewell banquet for him at the Café Voltaire, in the Place de l'Odéon. Gathered around Stéphane Mallarmé, were some thirty friends, symbolist poets and painters, or just friends (forty-five of them, according to Gauguin): Madame Rachilde and Alfred Valette, Jean Dolent, Charles Morice, Jean Moréas, Albert Aurier, Saint-Pol, Roux, Odilon, Rodin, Sérusier, Maurice Barrès, Daniel de Monfreid, and the only one of the whole assembly to have been decorated, Eugène Carrière. 'First of all, let us drink to the return of Paul Gauguin, but not without expressing our admiration for his uncompromising conscience that has led him, at the height of his talent, to choose exile, in order to seek fresh inspiration in distant lands and within himself.' It was in these terms that Mallarmé phrased his final farewell to the artist, on the threshold of his Tahitian adventure. 'Verses, toasts, and the warmest tribute to me ...'

A performance was held at the Théâtre des Arts for the benefit of Gauguin and Verlaine. The programme included *Cherubin* by

149

PORTRAIT OF A YOUNG TAHITIAN GIRL. 1892.
Private Collection.

Charles Morice, 'a youthful aberration' according to the critics,
L'Intruse (The Trespasser) by Maeterlinck, some poems by Hugo,
Lamartine, Baudelaire, and *Le Courbeau* (the Raven) by Edgar Poe,
in a translation by Mallarmé. But the evening, arranged with the
best intentions, did not make Gauguin a penny the richer.

His friends had approached the Minister of Fine Arts on his behalf
and secured him an official mission 'so that the marine and hospital
staff out there, etc. will be at my service ... I also have a com-

HEAD OF A TAHITIAN GIRL. 1891–93.
Private Collection, U.S.A.

mission for a picture – for three thousand francs – when I come back.'
An additional, appreciable advantage was a thirty per cent reduction
that was given him on the ticket by the shipping line.

Charles Morice was apparently the witness of a moral weakening
on the part of Gauguin, and saw him weeping over 'the horror of
the sacrifice I am making, and which is irreversible'. 'Farewell dear
Mette, dear children, love me well. And when I return we will be
re-married. So it is a kiss of betrothal that I send you today.'

Gauguin expressed his aesthetic opinions on many occasions in public, but he never wrote them down and formulated them in a coherent theory, like Emile Bernard or Maurice Denis. His remarks should have been taken down, while he sat discussing with other artists, a cigarette between his lips, and freely lacing his coffee with brandy. This, in fact, is what Albert Aurier tried to do in a study on 'Paul Gauguin, or Symbolism in Painting', which appeared in the *Mercure de France* in March 1891. This text took the form of a manifesto, rather than an analysis of the artist's work. It was not so much a discussion of Gauguin's work as it was at that time, but what it aimed to be, had the artist been able to fulfil all his intentions.

This text shows us what Gauguin's ambitions were in five points.

'The work of art should be: 1) centred upon an idea, since the expression of the idea should be its only ideal.' This is where the new school differed from Impressionism, which had been no more than a development of realism, a plastic, concrete representation of what the eye saw. Gauguin had often avowed his desire to attempt 'everything', no longer to represent the world, but to express it, to turn his painting into a physical expression of his ideas in an artistic form.

He had first admired, then criticized the over-simple symbolism of Millet in his *Angelus* as well as that of Maurice Denis. Theirs was no more than an illustration of the idea, not a formal equivalent for it.

'The work of art should be: 2) symbolist, since it must express this idea in forms.' In this instance Aurier showed himself to be extraordinarily subtle, and perceptive. He did not write 'In images', which would have applied to Millet and Maurice Denis in their use of over-simplified symbols; he spoke of 'forms', and urged that painting should find a specific language, to utilize the specific power of colours and lines in order to give material substance to a thought.

'The work of art should be: 3) synthetist, since it should portray its forms and symbols according to a method that can be generally

MAHANA MAA — SATURDAY, OR SHOPPING DAY. 1892.
Atheneum Museum, Helsinki.

understood.' Herein lies the difficulty. Apart from using a summary form of symbolism (red as blood, blue as the sky, etc.) each artist tends to create his own personal vocabulary of forms and symbols, which the viewer must assimilate before being able to penetrate the artist's thought. Thus it is unlikely that pictorial symbolism could ever have attained a universal validity. Nevertheless it is remarkable that before 1891 Gauguin should have had the idea of a plastic language with universal validity. Despite varied attempts and fifty years of research, abstract art has still not succeeded in overcoming these difficulties and in fulfilling this ambition.

'The work of art should be: 4) subjective, since the object should never be considered as an object, as such, but something perceived by the subject.' Aurier and Gauguin were prophetic in this anticipation of modern art and even of abstract art. They already believed that nothing exists in art outside the idea invented by the artist, and the plastic and symbolic use he puts it to. The concept of individualism in art was to develop along these lines to an extreme degree, to the point where art was robbed of its universal validity and of the 'method that can be generally understood', envisaged by Aurier in the third paragraph of his manifesto. The two points are not easy to reconcile. Where the artist is subjective, it is difficult for him to achieve a form that is universally intelligible. It was a dream that was too marvellous to work. Gauguin came near to fulfilling it, but the spirit of his most important Tahiti works remains 'sensitive' rather than explicit. And in any case, what does it matter? When put into everyday terms, his theories might sound banal. But in the form he has given them, they become incomparably poetic.

'The work of art should (in consequence) be: 5) decorative, for true decorative painting as understood by the Egyptians, and very likely by the Greeks and the primitives, is nothing other than a manifestation of art that is at once subjective, synthetist, symbolist and the crystallization of an idea.' If I interpret Albert Aurier's thoughts aright, he maintains that the Egyptians knew how to incorporate ideas and symbols into their decorative painting, and thus by painting ideas and symbols the modern artist should arrive at works that have a decorative value. This argument is little short of tautological. Let us confine ourselves to establishing that, in purifying forms, design and colours, in order to give them greater symbolic force and to give more strength to his ideas, Gauguin arrived at a form of painting that might be regarded as decorative. In fact his painting did possess decorative qualities in so far as they fitted harmoniously into the general structure, but it was fundamentally different from purely decorative painting in so far as it was primarily an expression of ideas and a personal conception of the world and of life.

This manifesto is a combination of intense individualism and a concern for universal comprehension which would make of the artist a sort of prophet, saint and messiah, a superman capable of inspiring his fellows with a personal vision that would be universally valid. It was Gauguin's profoundest ambition to achieve this aim, and he was to fulfil it accidentally with his exotism, thereby for a short while achieving an objective that might have appeared unattainable.

THE ENCHANTED ISLE

'During the night of 6th June, after sixty-three days sailing, sixty-three days of feverish waiting, and impatient daydreams about the yearned-for land—we caught sight of strange zig-zagging fires on the sea. A black jagged-edged cone stood out against the dark sky.

'We were passing Moorea and had sighted Tahiti.

'At first sight there was nothing fairy-like about this little island, nothing to compare with my magnificent bay of Rio de Janeiro, for example...'

It is in these poetic terms that Gauguin recaptured his arrival on Tahiti in his book Noa Noa. It is still a matter of some dispute today whether the boat on which he had booked his passage left Marseilles on 1st or 4th April. He regretted not having gone third class instead of second, as it would have been almost as comfortable and much cheaper. After calling at Suez, Aden and Mahé, the boat reached Australia at the end of April.

AHA OE FEII — WHAT, ARE YOU JEALOUS? 1892.
Hermitage Museum, Leningrad.

At Noumea in New Caledonia, thanks to his official mission, Gauguin was granted permission on 12th May to embark on a warship, 'La Vire', which was sailing on 21st May. Another eighteen days at sea and he would come to the end of his journey. Barely four days after his arrival Pomaré V, the last Tahitian king, died. The funeral rites were to last for a month, amidst extraordinary ceremonies.

It was little more than a century earlier that western men had first set foot on the island. It became the scene of bitter rivalries between English Protestant and French Catholic missionaries. To put an end to the disturbances, Pomaré accepted French protection and then consented to the status of a colony, on condition that his own privileges would be safe-guarded until his death.

In the French classic *Le mariage de Loti*, Loti the author had already foreseen that Tahitian traditions would come to an end with the accession of Pomaré, and Gauguin now witnessed a further stage in their eclipse with the disappearance of the last sovereign. The Catholic clergy, the gendarmes, the judges and the administrators did all they could to make the native people appear civilized, including all the hypocrisy contained in that word.

Gauguin was struck by the contrast between the western clothing of the French officials and the grass-skirts of the Maoris, who lived from day to day, with no care for the future, and he lost no time in taking the part of the 'noble savage'. He felt that this antithesis was stupid and unreasonable on an island such as this, lost in the heart of the Pacific, thousands of miles from the nearest continent.

When he was received by Governor Lacascade, who came from Martinique and enforced racial segregation, Gauguin found himself placed in a false position. He, the anarchistic artist, living in defiance of society, opposed to all academic institutions and all conventions, took his role as an official very seriously. The consideration and respectful attention, that had so long been denied him in Europe and which suddenly greeted him here, flattered him and during the first days he felt no qualms in maintaining such artificial relationships. He hoped to earn his living from a few allowances and by painting portraits of the wives of the high-ranking officials. But the promises that had been made him were soon forgotten. There was nothing to be gained by bowing to conventions that were even stranger and more absurd here than in Paris. And so Gauguin put disappointment and bitterness behind him – they had been mistaken about him just as he, himself, had been taken in by the pretences of colonial society and had allowed his natural sociability to be exploited.

Living in a native dwelling behind the cathedral of Papeete, Gauguin abandoned himself to the climate of the island, its inhabitants, their activities and their customs, and as was his habit, at first he drew more than he painted.

Gauguin learned the language of the country. He was astonished that so few words were adequate. 'Ia orana' meant hullo, as well as goodbye and thank you. He was particularly amused by the natives' constant use of the word 'onatu', which seemed to sum up their whole philosophy: 'I don't care', 'it doesn't matter', *après moi le déluge!*

Life in Papeete was expensive. Moreover the unspoiled ways of the Maoris and the earthly paradise, in search of which he had come, were not to be found here. So he moved to the district of Mataïea, about thirty miles from the capital, on the south coast of the island. Initial contacts with the Maoris proved difficult. They would watch him from a distance without ever approaching, and their attitude of nonchalance and indifference made Gauguin suddenly feel shy. However he needed their help in order to learn to live the way they did. By painting the portrait of one of the women he immediately gained the sympathy and the support of the little village. He no longer had to climb trees to pick *maïore*, the fruit of the breadfruit tree, with its horrible taste, and he now benefitted from the men's fishing.

Gauguin, delighted at every new discovery, was unrestrained in his enthusiasm. 'These people roam everywhere, go to any village, no matter where, sleep in a house, eat there, etc. without even saying thank you, all on the principle that they do the same for others. They sing, never steal, my door is always open, and they never kill.' Nevertheless he felt lonely, especially as he had only a limited knowledge of the language. He sent for a half-caste girl, nicknamed 'Titi' (ragamuffin), whom he had known in Papeete, but she was too westernized for his liking. She was of no help to him in making the sort of contact he was looking for, and he very soon sent her back where she had come from. Besides he was by then feeling sufficiently confident to live amongst the natives. He was no longer alone there.

MAIL FROM EUROPE

Gauguin did not forget Europe, and Europe did not entirely forget him. During the years he stayed in Tahiti, he wrote a great deal. Not only did he write a number of texts that are of major importance in an approach to his biography and for an interpretation of his work, such as *Noa Noa*, but he also kept up a regular correspondence with his wife, and with numerous friends, especially Daniel de Monfreid. The eighty-four letters, treasured and faithfully preserved by his friend, and published with unusual care by Madame Joly-Segalen, are the most poignant record in existence of his life in Tahiti and the sufferings he endured during the last years of his life. The book begins with a *Tribute to Paul Gauguin* by Victor Segalen, who assessed Gauguin's place in his own age, and in the history of art, and helps us to a better understanding of the man, his work, and the spirit that runs through these letters. Victor Segalen, who sailed the South Sea in the early years of this century at the time when Gauguin had taken refuge on the Marquesas Islands had been present at the sale that followed his death, and had been able to collect information regarding the circumstances in which he lived. We shall repeatedly refer to these letters to give an immediate authenticity to the great days of Gauguin's life.

In his letters Gauguin rarely dealt with problems of art. When he spoke about painting, it was to describe a canvas he had just finished, for the most recent work was always the one dearest to his heart. In some instances it was to help his friends identify works that he had shipped to Europe. More often it was to enquire whether one of them had not been sold, or to suggest prices, criticize them, suggest possible deliveries, and to work out what he might earn from further sales if they could be made. In short, what Gauguin talks about most in his letters is money – the money he is short of, the money he needs, money he is waiting for, and what he will do with it. It must be said that for an artist whose profession is not writing, and whose means of expression lies in the very special medium of painting, a letter is not the place for profound statements or aesthetic declarations, but simply a means of communication whereby he can settle material problems. This excuses and explains the occasionally somewhat disappointing nature of Gauguin's correspondence.

In March 1892, about a year after Gauguin's departure, he was compelled to remind his Parisian friends rather urgently of his

TE AA NO AREOIS — THE SEED OF THE AREOIS. 1892.
William S. Paley Collection.

existence. The funds he had brought with him were exhausted, and he sent out cries for help. He did not beg, he simply asked that the promises made to him should be kept, and that he should be sent what was owing to him.

In his letters to his wife he expressed constant anxiety about the children: 'I have been waiting for news, just a few words to show I am not forgotten. But nothing!', and he protests: 'Do not think me selfish and that I am abandoning you. But allow me some time to live in this way ... He attempts to justify himself: 'You tell me I am wrong to stay so far from the artistic centre. No, I am right, I have known for a long time what I am doing, and why. My artistic centre is in my brain and nowhere else, and I am strong because I am not distracted by others and because I do what is within me ...' 'I have an aim, and I pursue it constantly and gather material. Admittedly, every year there are transformations, but they all lead further along the same road. I alone am logical. That is why I find there are few who can follow me for long ... The conditions under which I am working are most unfavourable, and one needs to be a colossus to do what I am doing under such conditions.'

Gauguin displayed exceptional lucidity. Every time he undertook something, he was severely criticized, but the interest that was already being shown in his Breton period and which had taken material form at the sale held before his departure, proved to him that time was on his side, and would ultimately prove him right. This gave him grounds for hope and confidence in the future. But what strength of character he must have had in order to persist in his work, at a time when everything seemed to be conspiring to discourage him!

'I am waiting every month for money from Morice, with whom I left some, as well as the proceeds from a few outstanding pictures, but I have had neither money nor news of him ...'

He urged Mette to try to sell his works in Denmark: 'The more you sell, the more money you will get, and the more you can count on a brighter future. For one buyer leads to another. You for your part must work at this and get people used to buying. The Danish clientele is not to be despised ... It only needs the whim of one rich and influential man to launch a painter. Do you know what Claude Monet earns today? Around one hundred thousand francs a year.'

Mette was to act upon this advice. Gauguin sent her numerous pictures of Tahiti, but she never sent him the smallest part of the proceeds. He felt the lack of this money sorely, when he was overtaken by misfortune.

In the spring of 1892 he had a rather alarming heart attack. 'I have been very seriously ill. Imagine spitting up blood, a quarter of a litre a day without being able to stop; mustard plasters on my legs, and cupping on my chest, nothing helped. The hospital doctor was rather alarmed, and thought I was done for. My chest was unharmed and even quite strong, according to him; it's apparently my heart that's playing tricks on me. It's taken such a beating, that it's hardly surprising. I have been treated with digitalis, and here I am back on my feet again ...', he wrote to Daniel de Monfreid with some restraint.

The version he gave his wife was more dramatic, and by comparing the two versions we gain an interesting insight into Gauguin's character. With Monfreid, whose sympathy was a matter of course, he made no attempt to dwell on his own distress. However when it came to his wife, whom he knew to be reserved, he endeavoured to make himself appear interesting and to arouse pity for himself, at the same time trying to gain her admiration for his courageous attitude: 'Suddenly I started vomiting whole bowls full of blood. They treated me in hospital at twelve francs a day. You know me, I couldn't stay there at that expense. The chief forbade me outright from leaving, saying that he regarded me as lost if I were to do so. It appears that my heart had suffered severe injuries, which is hardly surprising. All the same, I did leave the hospital, and I have not had a relapse.'

These extracts illustrate the difficulties encountered by the historian anxious to get at the exact truth. With Gauguin the same event is often presented quite differently, depending on to whom he is describing it. It would not be true to say that he was putting on an act, but whether it was a conscious attempt or not, he always tried to find the formula that was likely to have the most effect, and which corresponded most closely to the part he was trying to play.

MARRIAGE TAHITIAN STYLE

For Gauguin the figure of a European returning to the healthy primitivism of native life was an ideal, which he never managed to attain – in the end it killed him. He brought this unattainable dream to life

163

in *Noa Noa*, words meaning 'perfumed land', referring to Tahiti. *Noa Noa* is the counterpart to *Le mariage de Loti*, less romantic and more poetic, and possibly more authentic, for in narrating his adventures he rarely romanticized them, but only embellished them. There is a long history attached to the manuscript of *Noa Noa*, and in order to trace it we are compelled to depart from chronological order, since the episodes from Gauguin's life in Tahiti contained in it took place during 1891 and 1892. The text was not published until 1897, when it appeared in *La Revue Blanche*, and in book form by *La Plume* in 1901. René Huyghe takes the credit for having unravelled the tangle of dates and successive additions by Gauguin and Charles Morice to the original text, when he was work-

TAPERA MAHANA – SUNSET. 1892.

TE MATETE — THE MARKET. 1892.
Kunstmuseum, Basle.

ing on the publication of another text by Gauguin, entitled *L'ancien culte Mahorie* (sic) (The ancient Maori religion), which was incorporated in *Noa Noa*.

In August 1893 Gauguin brought a first manuscript back to Paris, which he read to Charles Morice. This text was to be a commentary on the works he was painting, and would make it easier to understand them. Charles Morice undertook to edit it and have it published; in the form of a work in alternating cantos, with poems in verse or prose written by Morice as a transition between the sections of pure narrative written by Gauguin.

When Gauguin returned to Tahiti, each of them kept a copy of the unfinished manuscript, and each author continued to work at it on his own, without consulting the other. Gauguin had almost finished his text, but he was revising it; Morice, for his part, was deleting and inserting additions of his own, and in short it was Morice's manuscript that was published, a manuscript in which Gauguin's original account had been considerably altered in order to arrive at a closer unity in the style.

Only one of the two original manuscripts of *Noa Noa* is known today. This is the one which Gauguin took back with him, and which was subsequently bequeathed to the Louvre by Daniel de Monfreid. Charles Morice had entrusted the other one to the care of Mette Gauguin and was never able to recover it. It was he who did the groundwork for the later and so-called definitive edition, published in 1929 by G. Crès & Co., when Gauguin's original text was rediscovered. Only the initial pages, *La Mémoire et l'Imagination* and the first chapter *Songerie* (Reverie), and the poems are by Charles Morice. The first edition consisted of eleven chapters, of which only six were by Gauguin. There is also a noticeable difference in the style. Morice's affected writing, with its mannered phrasing so dear to the symbolists has dated, whereas the straightforward, compact and unadorned narrative of Gauguin has retained all its freshness.

Later the two men quarrelled over the authorship of the book. Gauguin made his position quite clear: 'I had the idea of contrasting the character of the non-civilized native with our own, and I thought it might be original for me to write in a simple, primitive style alongside something in a sophisticated style by Morice. I envisaged and arranged the collaboration between us with this in mind, and was also interested to find out, since I am not, as they say, in the trade, which of us would emerge as the better.'

The book portrays the landscape and the poetry of the 'perfumed isle', the simple and peaceful life of its inhabitants, the freedom of their customs, and the food on which they fed. The narrator goes back to his arrival there, his first contacts, his relationship with 'Titi', his first portrait of a Tahitian woman, and the first friendly overtures of the natives, and his relations with them. Chapter VI is entirely given up to his marriage to Tehura. Was this a genuine account? For the most part, it surely was.

'For some time I have been feeling very gloomy. My work is affected by it. Admittedly there are a lot of documents that have failed to turn up, but what I miss most is happiness.'

One day while on a tour of the island he burst out: 'Why go any further, aren't the girls here as pretty as any?' And without more ado, he was 'married'.

Tehura's first appearance had inspired him to write these lines: 'Through the extremely transparent pink muslin of the dress one could see the golden skin of her arms and shoulders. Her breasts stood out in two firm buds, and her charming face was different from the type that I had been accustomed to see everywhere until then. Her hair too was quite unusual, growing like a bush, and slightly crinkly. In the sunlight, the whole effect was an orgy of colours.'

After a final ceremonial libation, they set off, accompanied by the whole family, to the cheers of the village population. Only the wife of the gendarme exclaimed: 'What! Are you going off with a harlot?' And Gauguin's reaction was: 'there was something symbolic in the sight of these two women – here was decrepitude side by side with the bloom of youth, artifice next to nature, and on the latter the former blew an impure breath of spitefulness and falsehood.' This was an idea that he was to express in his painting.

'Here were two races face to face, and I was ashamed of my own. It seemed to me that it was sullying the beautiful sky with a cloud of dirty smoke. And I turned away quickly, and let my gaze rest upon and delight in the brilliance of this creature of living gold, with whom I was already in love.'

It took just a week for Tehura to become accustomed to her new situation, and to bring to life the idyll the artist had been dreaming of. One day Gauguin had to go to Papeete. He came back at night. In the dark his hut seemed deserted, he rushed forward and struck a match ... 'Motionless, lying naked on the bed, stretched out flat on her stomach, her eyes wide with fear, Tehura was looking at me and

TE POIPOI – MORNING. 1892.
Mr and Mrs Charles S. Payson Collection, New York.

seemed not to recognize me. Tehura's terror was contagious, a phos-
phorescent light seemed to stream out of her eyes which were in a
fixed stare. I had never seen her look so beautiful, never so moving
in her beauty ... How can I know what I was for her at that
moment? With alarm on my face, she may well have taken me for
some of those demons or ghosts, those *tupapaus*, who fill the sleepless
nights of her people.'

This was the inspiration for that magnificent canvas, *Manao Tupapau*–'the spirit of the dead watches'. The attitude of the Tahitian
girl's body on the milky, pale sheet, the intensity and at the same

time the abstraction in her look of terror, it is all there, while behind in the lefthand corner we do not know whether the roughly drawn silhouette is that of a Tupapau, or of Gauguin himself, as he appeared to Tehura on that night.

He attached great importance to this canvas, which he was anxious 'to keep or sell for a high price'. He commented on it himself in the following words: '... a nude of a young girl. In this posture, just a trifle, and she would be indecent. But this is the way I want her, I am interested by the lines and the movement. Then I have made her look a bit frightened. The excuse if not the explanation for this fear is in the character of the Maori. There is a very strong tradition among this people that makes them fear the spirits of the dead. A young girl in our world would be terrified at being seen in such a posture. Not so with this woman, her fear is something I have to explain by concise literary means, as they used to do formerly. And so this is what I have done.

'General harmony, sombre, melancholy, and frightening like the sound of a funeral knell. Purple, dark blue and orange-yellow. The linen is greenish-yellow 1) because native linen is quite different from that which we use (beaten bark of a tree), 2) because it suggests the artificial light (Kanak women never sleep in the dark), without the effect of lamplight (which is commonplace), and 3) this yellow, linking the orange-yellow and the blue, completes the musical accord. There are some flowers in the background, but they do not have to be realistic, since they are imaginary, and I make them look like sparks. For the Kanaka the phosphorescence at night represents the spirits of the dead, they believe in them, and are afraid of them. In the end I make the ghost simply a good little woman, because this girl has no knowledge of the performances of French spiritualists, and can only imagine the spirit of death, as death itself, namely a person like herself ... To finish, the painting has to be executed very simply, the keynote being savage and childish.'

This commentary differs from that chapter in *Noa Noa* dealing with the same canvas. There are two reasons for this — firstly, he was writing to his wife, which explains his reticence; or on the other

TAHITIAN GIRLS. 1891–93.

hand, it may have been intended to give him an opportunity of answering the probing questions of amateurs or critics, and was written later. In the first instance, Gauguin does not refer to the original event, and confines his remarks to its pictorial rendering; in the second case, however, he departs from the picture itself, and explains to the observer the origin of its inspiration. Gauguin very lucidly divides his explanation into two parts—first he emphasizes the emotional and evocative value of the colour, then he goes on to

EA HAERE IA OE – WHERE ARE YOU GOING? 1893.
Hermitage Museum, Leningrad.

show how this is supported by the emotion aroused by the model.

It is a pity that he did not refer to the design and its symbolic power. The slight angle formed by the body is just sufficient to dispel the impression of repose conveyed by all horizontal lines, and in particular by a body lying stretched out. Furthermore, the vertical shape of the dark silhouette, echoed by the beam against which it is leaning, adopts a menacing position in the composition. This is no friend looking on benevolently, but a shade that is watching. But the success of such a picture was not entirely a conscious effort, and there are some effects which Gauguin achieved which were not the product of reasoned logic.

In *Noa Noa* Gauguin dwelt at length on the beliefs of the Tahitians, and he attempted to give an account of their mythology. Tehura had divulged the secrets of her gods to him. Taaora and Jesus appeared to be curiously mingled in her mind. The missionaries had superimposed their form of worship, but they had not succeeded in eliminating paganism. Tehura went to the temple or to church, but she knew nothing about Christian ethics. The Tahitians already possessed a developed knowledge of astrology and Gauguin admired Tehura's interest in the stars and what she told him about them.

Certain biographers have claimed that the ancient Maori worship had long since disappeared when Gauguin came to the island, and that Tehura could not have been familiar with them. They accused Gauguin of having plagiarized a work by Mr Moerenhout, who had been United States Consul in Tahiti at the time of the Pritchard affair and had been in charge of French interests on the island. His book, *Travels in the Islands of the Great Ocean*, appeared in 1837. Jacques-Antoine Moerenhout did in fact have the opportunity of meeting one of the last 'harepos', those Tahitian priests who were responsible for the preservation of the ancient legends by oral tradition. But the missionaries had suppressed them, just as they had insisted on the burial of the last idols or 'tikis' in the forests.

Gauguin attributed his discovery of Tahitian mythology to Tehura, but he did not deny that he had gathered information from Moerenhout's work, and in *Noa Noa* he declared: 'I am adding to Tehura's teaching with the help of information found in a collection by Moerenhout, the former consul. I am obliged to M. Goupil, a settler in Tahiti, for letting me read this edition.'

After having related the Polynesian version of the creation and the theory of evolution, which in the mind of the natives was linked

PORTRAIT OF THE ARTIST WITH IDOL. 1893.
Arthur Sachs Collection.

to the transformation of the world, Gauguin adds: 'Unity of matter, the theory of evolution, who would have thought the philosophy of these former cannibals would contain the evidence of such an advanced culture? And yet there is nothing that I have added. Moerenhout's good faith cannot be disputed.' This clears Gauguin of an unjust accusation of plagiarism.

In *Noa Noa* he traces the origins of cannibalism among the Areois to a curious legend, and justifies it as the concern for survival of a prolific race, living in an island of limited resources.

These legends, which he examined in *Noa Noa*, do not reappear in any explicit form in Gauguin's painting, which was only receptive to tangible manifestations of thought.

FIRST REFLECTIONS OF A NEW WORLD

During this period Gauguin's life was a harmonious mingling of fact and fiction. He saw everything in pictorial terms; his vision was realistic enough, but seemed to belong to another world, a universe where life was simple, ideal, idyllic, and full of mystery, as if in communion with the divine.

One of his first large Tahitian canvases was *Ia orana Maria* (page 121), a sort of Tahitian Epiphany. There is no doubt that the woman and the child she bears on her shoulders are holy figures, and this is born out by the haloes around their heads. In the background are two figures with hands folded expressing adoration, and a winged figure clad in a pink robe, a Polynesian angel. A deep serenity emanates from this composition, in which the figures are in perfect harmony with nature around them, they belong to it and appear to fuse into one with it. The fruit in the foreground, the earth that goes from yellow to pink, the touches of dark green foliage that merge into the dark blue of the mountain, everything contributes to the same movement, and to the same harmony.

This perfect harmonising of the new world with his own style was not something Gauguin achieved right away, but only after numerous attempts. His early figures were clothed. He did not hesitate to modulate these broad areas of coloured cloth with ample movements, thus departing from the rigid principles of cloisonnism, as in *The Women of Tahiti*, or *Parau Parau – Words, Words* (page 145), which date from 1891. He even returned to a timid form of Impressionism in one of his first Tahitian canvases, *Te tiare Farani – The Flowers of France* (page 136), which is a composition of classical complexity. However, his whole development was to move towards extreme simplification, which was to be the strength of his work.

For a few more months he continued to arrange his Tahitian landscapes in the same way as his Breton ones. In *Nafea foa ipoipo – When will you be married?* (page 148) there is still the gently undulating landscape, the range of colours produced by parallel close-etched strokes, and the oblique line formed by the tree trunk. The exotic elements have been planted as a decorative or symbolic addition to a landscape that has little of the exotic about it. These reddish or yellowish palm trees suspended in space are out of place in this setting, they do not become an integral part of their surroundings, until they are highly stylized.

Paradoxically, it is the realistic features that seem artificial, but once they are reduced to the form of pure and perfectly unrealistic symbols, they spring to life and become more natural, because they have become absorbed into the canvas by an inner logic. With his second year in Tahiti, the palms and flowers that appear in the pictures painted in 1892 are no more than stylizations and the waves and reflections in the water have taken on purely decorative shapes, like those in Japanese engravings. But now they are no longer intrusive, because they do not mar the harmony of the picture, they contribute to the general impression sought by the artist in his composition.

In *Aha oe feii – What, are you jealous?* (page 156) everything, from the stylized reflections in the water in the lefthand corner to the all-over pale white tone of the sand, barely turned to pink by the heat, everything serves to emphasize the counterpoint between the two bodies, the subtle contrast between the bronze tint of the body that is seen from the front, and in the shade, and the yellow, burnt ochre tone of the breast fully exposed to the sun. In a work

SIESTA. 1894.
Ira Haupt Collection, New York.

such as this, all is suggestion, though nevertheless indicated with perfect precision. Even the unusual angle from which the figures are seen is not fortuitous, as happens in photography; it has been calculated quite deliberately, and not arrived at by intuition; on the one hand, this arrangement places the two bodies in opposition to each other, and on the other hand it manages to establish a unity between them, without any awkward distortion on the canvas.

Pictures dating from the same year, 1892, but probably painted in earlier months, *Te aa no Areois* (page 160), *Vaïrumati tei oa* (page 161) and *Te Matete—The Market* (page 165) illustrate the

176

difficulties which Gauguin had overcome in order to portray these wonderful bodies and incorporate them into his painting in an aesthetic and entirely personal way. The Tahitian women are arrested here in attitudes that irresistibly recall Egyptian frescoes and designs.

These archaeological reminiscences temporarily provided a simple and effective method of integrating the figures into their setting, and the result is striking. The stiffness of the postures contrasts with the sensuous proportions of the bodies, and creates a discord. The beautiful Tahitian women are shown in stylized poses alien to them, making them look as if they had been immobilized for centuries. This artificial setting, quite foreign to the South Seas, introduces us into an

NAVE NAVE MOE – THE JOY OF RESTING. 1894.
Hermitage Museum, Leningrad.

unreal world, a sort of paradise where splendid disorder reigns, and the free-and-easy and abandoned attitude of the voluptuous Tahitian women has suddenly fallen into line under the magic baton of a conductor, builder of pyramids.

With each new canvas there is increasing evidence of Gauguin's great triumph in the field of colour. In his earliest Tahitian works he hesitated in the use of broken, subdued colours, but he could not yet introduce the true, brilliant colours into his painting without upsetting the harmony. Gradually he became bolder and extended his use of pure colours to areas of increasing size, but never more than one such colour in any one canvas. His work could not tolerate two such violent elements without breaking up into an explosion of colour. He was to await a self-evident truth, by totally 'symbolising' colour.

His landscapes became more real once he had transposed them. They were no longer an image approaching reality without ever reaching it, but became a perfectly homogeneous plastic equivalent of reality, which recreated the atmosphere experienced in a certain place, without attempting to reproduce it faithfully either in detail or in colour. Their truth lay in their poetry, their related tones, and in the harmony of their different parts, placed as they were on the canvas by the magic of Gauguin's talent.

How remote is the *Tahiti Landscape* of 1891 from this intimate scene, discreetly dubbed *Te Poipoi–Morning* (page 168), with the woman's dress a vivid splash of red, revealing as she crouches the dark bronze of her skin! In the first there are the somewhat stiff silhouettes, and in the second a stylization that conveys the life and movement of a posture without upsetting the peaceful arrangement of the picture. The landscape in *Morning* has none of the turbulent contrasts of the first painting; it is all in closely related shades of colour, and similar tones, blues shading to browns by way of greens. It is a close complex of overlapping shapes and colours that suddenly come alive because the artist was able to dominate and keep in check the magical power of these colours.

Gauguin had every reason to be proud of himself and to write: 'I have worked hard all this time, and there are now 40 metres of canvas covered with Lefranc & Company's colours. I feel I have really hit on something, and it would have been a shame to leave' (he had been thinking of returning to France). 'I have just finished the head of a Kanaka, arranged against a white cushion in a palace of my own invention and attended by women who are also of my own invention.' He told his wife: 'I now have thirty-two canvases, one of which is 3 metres by 1 metre 30, three are 1 metre 20 by 90 and the remainder by 70. Quite a number of drawings and sketches, and several bits of carving.'

It had taken him several visits to Brittany over several years before he had produced his Breton period – but after barely a year's residence in Tahiti in complete freedom, he was already producing his first masterpieces, although he had set himself the task of conveying a natural landscape, a light and people that were totally different from those he had known and had hitherto used as models.

In the canvases he painted in 1893 prior to his return to Europe, he displayed even more boldness and mastery in his colour contrasts and the unusual but tremendously significant arrangement of the composition. *Siesta* (page 176) and *The Source of Light* attained a degree of purity and symbolic power hitherto unknown in western painting. This progress had not been achieved without its doubts and anxiety about how he was to exist and continue to paint.

In March 1892 he was still only just beginning to grasp the Tahitian nature, as is born out by his letters to Daniel de Monfreid. 'I live like a savage now, I go about naked except for the vital parts, which women don't like to see (so they say). I am doing more and more work, but until now only studies or rather records, which are piling up. If they don't help me, they may be of use to other people later on. However I have done one painting, an angel with yellow wings showing two Tahitian women, half-dressed in pareos, a sort of flowered cotton fabric that is worn as you like and hangs from the waist, the figures are Maria and Jesus, who are also Tahitians. Very dark mountain background and trees in flower – dark violet path and foreground emerald green; with bananas on the left – I am very pleased with it.'

MAHANA NO ATUA – THE DAY OF GOD. 1894.
Art Institute of Chicago.

This was the picture of *Ia orana Maria* (page 121), which marks the splendid beginning of his great Tahitian period. Gauguin's strength lay in his refusal to yield to the temptation of throwing the colours on at random; he always reflected at great length before setting to work, and when he took up his brushes he knew exactly what he wanted to say and how he would express it.

ABANDONED BY HIS PARISIAN FRIENDS

When Gauguin left Paris in March 1891, his friends had been full of reassuring promises of expected sales and money that would be sent on to him. Moreover, several of the canvases bought had not yet been paid for. Charles Morice was made responsible for collecting the money and sending it on to Gauguin. Now, one year later in 1892, entirely without resources Gauguin wrote not without some bitterness: 'It is now more than a year since I went away, and I now have more of a reputation than before, yet nothing has been sold, whereas when I was there, I always managed to raise two thousand francs or so. Nothing from Tanguy, Portier or Goupil. I just can't believe it.'

Charles Morice struck him an even more cruel blow, for this was a friend in whom he had placed his confidence. 'As for Morice! I have said goodbye to the money he has of mine and I am astonished by his silence and his behaviour.'

It was not surprising that he was losing heart. He even thought of giving up painting. There is an element of blackmail in his saying: 'When I think about it, I believe I shall have to give up painting on my return, since it cannot provide me with enough to live on. I left Paris after a victory, only a limited one, but a victory all the same. In eighteen months I have not seen a cent from my painting, which means I have sold less than before. The moral is fairly obvious.'

All this is untrue. Maurice Joyant, who had taken over from Theo van Gogh at the Boussod-Valadon gallery, had been working to good avail. He wrote him: 'You cannot imagine how the climate of opinion has changed . . .' and he sent him a sales sheet. Gauguin discovered that since May 1891 more than 800 francs had been remitted to Morice, who had failed to pass this on. 'Which means that Morice has done me out of one thousand three hundred and fifty-three francs, which would have saved my life . . . I am bound to say I am staggered to learn of this theft. For that is what it amounts to.'

As a result of Morice's negligence, Gauguin had been compelled to live under deplorable conditions, which had begun to tell on him. 'Life is very expensive here, and I am ruining my health by not eating,' he lamented in letters to his wife, 'I have heard from Paris that you are counting on selling some canvases in Denmark. If you succeed with this deal, do try and send me just a small part of the proceeds. My health is getting worse because I eat so little. I still prefer that to giving up the struggle . . .'

APATARAO: QUARTER OF PAPEETE. 1893.
Ny Carlsberg Glyptothek, Copenhagen.

He now approached the governor with a view to being repatriated.
On the first occasion he met a captain who bought a canvas from
him for 400 francs, but this opportunity did not repeat itself. Administrative delays were to hold up his repatriation. The Minister for
Fine Arts had sent a favourable report from Paris, but had not issued
any official instructions! The local administration did not wish to
pay out, and asked Paris if the government would subsidize the cost
of the voyage. Eventually Gauguin left on his own account.

PEASANT AND HIS DOG. 1894.
Private Collection, Paris.

His wife did not help Gauguin any more than his friends did. Mette was selling some canvases, but considered the money these produced as her due, and had made it a principle never to send her husband any amount, however slight. It is true that she was responsible for five children and had to provide for them. When she learned of her husband's difficulties, she did not soften in her attitude. Gauguin was kept informed by Schuffenecker, who was in close correspondence with Mette. 'My wife has had another eight hundred and fifty francs from sales, but she is in need, and apologizes for not sending me any money. What can I do!'

The chief buyer was the director of *Politiken*, Edvard Brandès, who had married Ingeborg Gad, one of Mette's sisters, who had been divorced from the painter, Fritz Thaulow. Over the years he paid Mette close on 10,000 francs for the pictures in Gauguin's collection, to which were added a number of the artist's own works. Brandès claimed that he was buying these works in order to help Mette, but when in 1894 Gauguin wanted to buy the Cézanne back from him or to exchange it for one of his own recent works, Brandès dryly declined, saying he had become attached to his collection.

Mette, proud of the interest she had aroused, suggested to Gauguin that an exhibition might be arranged for him in Denmark. Flattered by the appreciation of northern collectors, Gauguin wanted this exhibition to give a complete picture of his development, and he sent nine canvases. He put them in the care of an artillery officer who was leaving for France. This person sent them in a big roll to Daniel de Monfreid, carriage forwarded, who in turn dispatched them to Copenhagen. This was a long journey for fragile works, and Gauguin was concerned about their condition. He asked Monfreid to examine them thoroughly, and if necessary to see to any repairs, and to wash and 'wax' them, and gave him further instructions, showing how much he valued them.

The selection was entirely representative, including nudes, landscapes, and characteristic or 'genre' figures, to use the correct term. He sent his wife and Daniel de Monfreid the list of paintings simultaneously. He insisted that only the Maori titles should appear in the catalogue, and only gave the translations as a guide. The choice is an excellent one: *Words, Words, The Spirit of the Dead Watches, What, are you jealous?, Parahi te Marae, Te Faaturuma, Te Rau Rahi,* (The great tree), *I Raro te Oviri* (Beneath the Pandanus), *Te Fare Maorie* (The Maori dwelling), and to these he asked Daniel de Monfreid to add a ninth canvas—*Vahine note tiare* (Woman with Blossom). Gauguin fixed the prices; he was determined that they should be higher than those of the French canvases, 600 francs minimum. As for *Manao Tupapau*, he proved how attached he was to it, by refusing to let it go for less than 1,500 or 2,000 francs.

DAVID'S MILL. 1894.
Louvre, Paris.

Two exhibitions were held simultaneously; one consisting of about fifty works, paintings, sculptures and ceramics was held in the Free Exhibition building, beginning on 26th March 1893, and the other opened on the same day at Kleis, in the March Exhibition, and included seven paintings and six ceramics.

These exhibitions were greeted not only by articles in the press, and particularly *Politiken*, but also by a number of important sales at fairly high prices. Was Mette going to prove to be her husband's best business agent? Her associates suggested she should organize an exhibition in London, where the public would be favourably disposed. But Mette was working for her own profit. In the end Gauguin had to accept the facts. In April, when he wanted more than ever to return to France, he stated that he could not take the warship that was leaving for Noumea on 1st May. He wrote simply: 'If you had sent the money for the last picture you would have saved my life ... You preferred to keep the money, I cannot reproach you, but it was desperately urgent.'

Luckily Daniel de Monfreid sent him some money, including, much to his surprise, 700 francs from Mette. Borrowing 400 francs against the canvases he left as a security, he assembled the necessary sum.

However it was the hour of reckoning. He wrote: 'I shall soon be a father again, in the South Seas. My God! It looks as if I have to sow my wild oats everywhere. Admittedly, it is not such a terrible thing here, children are welcomed, and claimed in advance by all the relations. They go to whoever wish to be the fosterparents. For you know in Tahiti the best present you can make anyone is to give them a child. So I am not unduly perturbed about its fate.'

Mette had told him in some detail about the lives of their elder children, and he spoke of them with pride and joy at the thought of seeing them again. He admitted bitterly that he had aged, his hair was going white, and his features were hollow, and that he looked older than his age. But: 'In the two years I have spent here, with only a few months lost, I have produced sixty-six more or less fine canvases and a number of ultra-primitive sculptures. That is enough for any one man.'

Gauguin's two periods in Tahiti were separated by an interval of two years spent in France, from 30th August 1893 when he arrived in Marseilles without a penny in his pocket until his departure from the same port on 3rd July 1895. It was a particularly lively period – he painted little, but was engaged in great activity. He was to exhibit at the Impressionist dealer's, Durand-Ruel, without reaping any of the material profits that should have accompanied his growing fame. Sundry unfortunate incidents – a leg broken in Brittany, the betrayal of his mistress Annah, the Javanese girl, the final break with his wife, unsuccessful court cases, and the ill-will of the public authorities – would decide him to return to the tropics.

Paul Gauguin was about to embark on a decisive phase of his existence. His bad luck began with the journey back to France. At Noumea he waited twenty-five days for the boat for Europe. The ship was packed with three hundred soldiers, and the third class was so overcrowded that he had to pay the additional amount and go second class. There was a spell of bad weather. He suffered from the cold at Sydney and from the scorching heat on the Red Sea. 'So much so,' he recorded, 'that we have thrown three men overboard who died from the heat.' Fortunately, Daniel de Monfreid had sent him a letter poste restante to Marseilles, enabling him to secure a little money in order to reach Paris. First he put up at his friend's studio, and then he borrowed enough money from the proprietress of the little bistro in the rue de la Grande-Chaumière, opposite the Academy Colarossi, to rent a studio at no. 8 in the same street.

Gauguin had regained his health and put on weight during the boat trip. He felt ready to tackle Paris. The summer was barely over when he eagerly began renewing former contacts. He paid a short visit to Orleans to attend the funeral of his uncle Isidore, and returning with hopes centred on his expected inheritance, prepared a big exhibition of his recent paintings.

On the recommendation of Edgar Degas, Durand-Ruel, the important dealer, visited his studio to inspect the canvases he had

NAVE, NAVE FENUA. c. 1895.

THE LAST SUPPER. 1899.
Katia Granoff Collection, Paris.

brought back from Tahiti, and agreed to exhibit them. Gauguin believed his triumph to be close at hand, and intended to leave nothing undone that might make it complete. He now plunged himself into the expense of printing a catalogue. Meanwhile he had seen Charles Morice. Exactly what took place at their first meeting is not known – it was probably taken up with violent reproaches on the one side, and excuses and explanations on the other. Morice's justifications for his behaviour must have been convincing, for it was he who wrote the introduction for Gauguin's catalogue. In it he drew a portrait of the artist and set out the reasons for his going to Tahiti: '...it may seem astounding that a painter, particularly a creative artist such as he, should need to look beyond our own familiar scene for inspiration for his creativity ... Gauguin did not go out there to find new subjects to refresh his mind. Gauguin, perhaps more than any other, could content himself indefinitely with the same place or the same face, and would be able to present it each time in a fresh interpretation, hitherto unseen. But apart from his qualities of personal and lively inventiveness and profound intuition, his lack of reserve, his expansiveness, and his complete openness make him dislike the narrow life and the artificial ostentation of our western civilization.

'He has no patience for our customs, our prejudices, our conventions in art and in everything, and our imitative tradition that has such an oppressive hold on painting in particular ... What has driven him so far afield is the desire to forget us and his prime concern for his own preference in painting ... As a decorative painter, he has recalled this unique form of decoration, and has brought it back for us to see.'

In his poetic way, Charles Morice brought out the personality of the man – here were the early beginnings of the myth which was built up by poets and friends of the artist!

The exhibition consisted of forty-six items – a prodigious collection, among which there were a number of masterpieces, such as *Ia orana Maria, Manao Tupapau, Tahitian Pastorales, What, are you jealous?, When will you be married?, Woman with a Blossom,*

Woman with Mangoes, several landscapes, a few canvases of Brittany, including *Bonjour Monsieur Gauguin,* and two sculptures.

Mette had to be asked several times before she would consent to sending back those Tahitian paintings from the Copenhagen exhibition that had remained unsold – the two which Gauguin considered to be the finest were missing. Exasperated at this, Gauguin insisted that Mette supply him with an exact account of which paintings were still in her possession, and which ones she had sold. Fortunately his preoccupation with the exhibition distracted him from his growing resentment. Before the varnishing-day, on 4th November, he still had to mount and frame his canvases, touch up those that had been damaged in transit, and finally coat them with a thin film of wax, a particular habit of his.

Alas, contrary to all expectations, the Parisian public understood neither the symbolism of the work, nor the poetry of the Polynesian landscapes and people. They visited the exhibition as they would a circus, they came for entertainment, to laugh and jeer at the sight of these specimens of an unfamiliar race, and were struck by their animal nature rather than by their natural purity. The colours appeared crude, the design clumsy, and the intention incomprehensible.

Chagrined and disappointed, Gauguin explained himself somewhat testily, simplifying his ideas in the briefest terms, to show his contempt for the reactionary attitude of this public, that regarded itself as the most sophisticated in the world. 'Since I wanted to suggest a profuse and luxuriant vegetation, and a sun that sets everything aflame I had to present my people in a corresponding setting.

'Of course this is the outdoor life, but yet it is intimate, with its thickets, its shaded streams, and these women whispering in a vast palace decorated by Nature with all the riches Tahiti possesses.

'Hence all these fabulous colours, this sultry yet subdued and silent atmosphere.'

He also attempted to explain the mystery that seemed to envelope his portraits of Tehura.

'She is extremely subtle, and very knowing in her naïvety, this Tahitian Eve. The enigma that lies in the depth of her childlike eyes

BRETON GIRL AT PRAYER. 1894.
Mrs Augusta McRoberts Collection, England.

is something that seems to me impossible to convey. This is no pretty Rarahou, listening to a pretty ballad by Pierre Loti, prettily playing the guitar. This is Eve after the fall, who can still walk naked and hold her head up high without shame, retaining all her animal beauty as on the first day.

'Like Eve, the body has remained animal. But the head has changed and developed, thought has produced subtlety, love has printed an ironic smile on the lips, and naïvely, she searches in her

WASHERWOMEN. 1894.
Robert MacKay Collection, New York.

memory for the explanation of the present day. Enigmatically, she looks at you.'

For all that, people would not be won over. The public in 1893 admired officially recognized painting, like that of Meissonier or Bonnat, whose subjects illustrated their own philosophy and reassured them. When pressed, they could accept the effects of light, the poetry, and the audacious use of colour of the Impressionists. But they considered painting should be the representation of the beauti-

193

ful, they could not accept that art could be anything else, that it could become a means of expression, that it could contain a philosophy of life, and that it could be the reflection of individual and personal lyricism.

The opposition to Gauguin at this exhibition fell into different factions. The press was for the most part hostile, with the exception of those who were friends of the artist, like Charles Morice or Octave Mirbeau. Certain papers, however, only maintain their circulation by faithfully reflecting the opinions of the majority of their readers. Also against Gauguin were old Impressionists, like Pissarro, who was disappointed by the development of his one-time disciple, as well as being opposed on principle to the subjective nature of symbolism in painting. Monet and Renoir largely shared his point of view: Impressionism possessed ample means of portraying the atmosphere and its countless variations, as well as the shimmer of light on flesh, without it being necessary to resort to anything else.

Alone among the Impressionists was the solitary old Degas, who had always responded to the human character, and to the power of Gauguin's treatment, and he displayed his esteem not merely in words, but by purchase. Also violently in favour of Gauguin, and always ready to give noisy expression to their approval, was the entire Nabis group, and Bonnard and Vuillard in particular. The young artists of this group regarded the exhibition as a manifesto. Equally in favour were a few wealthy art-lovers, who were willing to pay a high price for the painting of their choice, such as M. Manzi, who paid 2,000 francs for *Ia orana Maria*.

Before the exhibition opened, Gauguin had never dreamed that it could be anything but a success, and he had raised his prices sharply, asking up to 3,000 francs (equivalent to approximately £550 today) for some canvases which he regarded as especially important. This may have deterred the less courageous of buyers.

Gauguin was deeply affected by this defeat–he had sold no more than about ten paintings, and the press had turned out against him– and this new disappointment influenced his subsequent behaviour.

194

Along with the troubles he was encountering over his exhibition, Gauguin was conducting an epistolary battle with his wife.

Ever since his return, she had been, as we saw, extremely unwilling to return the Tahitian pictures that he wished to exhibit in Paris. His uncle Isidore's legacy was to increase the bad feelings between them. Mette was expecting to receive the children's share. Gauguin himself had led her to expect as much: 'My uncle's death will put everything straight...' To begin with there was politeness on either side. The prospect of the money put both partners in a good mood. Gauguin complained that his wife had not come to Paris with the children to see him on his return from Tahiti. He offered to pay her the cost of the journey out of the inheritance. But Mette did not wish to take any chances – she did not trust him. However she suggested that her husband should come and see them, but he did not want to leave on account of the exhibition, and later he declined the invitation, alleging he was too occupied with various matters, such as receptions and visits from purchasers. Mette began to lose patience, and accused Gauguin of keeping all the money from the legacy for himself, whereas in fact the lengthy procedures involved in settlement of an inheritance were alone to blame. Indeed, Gauguin's sister, Marie was a joint beneficiary, and he needed to obtain power of attorney from her husband, Juan Uribe, who was in Panama. 'The lawyer is being extremely slow,' he explained, 'and meanwhile I have to keep putting off the repayment of small sums I borrowed on the understanding that I would repay them by October.'

Mette was not satisfied with this explanation. She accused Gauguin, and he defended himself: 'Can you imagine that if I had any money, I should not have sent you some?' In desperation, he sent her a detailed account of his expenses. The amount of his inheritance was unconfirmed. Gauguin mentioned 9,000 francs in his letters to his wife, but later spoke of 13,000 francs to Monfreid.

Gauguin added up all the expenses of his stay in Marseilles, the cost of his railway ticket to Paris, his rent, the freight charges on

195

the pictures that had been sent back from Copenhagen, his purchases of linen and bedding, medical fees, the cost of his journey to Orleans, his food, tobacco, and indispensable items of clothing, right down to the inevitable heading of 'sundry expenses' ... His heaviest expenses were for frames and stands for his exhibition – 750 francs, the publication of the catalogue – 125 francs, and the 400 francs sent back to Tahiti, which he had borrowed in order to return to Europe. The total came to about 2,500 francs.

Thus he refused to send Mette the 4,500 francs she had been asking for. He deducted the 2,500 francs for his expenses and declared: 'Half of seven thousand five hundred francs is not four thousand five hundred francs!' ... 'It is extraordinary that I should be com-

TE ARII VAHINE – WOMAN WITH MANGOES. 1896.
Pushkin Museum, Moscow.

BABY. 1896.
Hermitage Museum, Leningrad.

pelled to send you my accounts, and to persuade you that I need to live elsewhere than in the street, and that with my sickness that comes from living in a hot climate, I cannot walk about quite naked and that I have to keep warm.'

We do not know exactly what Mette replied, but it is not difficult to guess. She used all the arguments at her disposal in favour of the children, to prevent her husband from squandering his inheritance. But Gauguin, who still remembered his own vain appeals for help

197

when he was ill in Tahiti and bitterly recalled certain phrases from his wife's letters, refused to listen to her: 'As you told me not long ago, I must manage on my own (I am only too well aware of that) and on what? With my products (you have them all). I shall take steps to see that in the future I shall never be faced with what happened to me when I arrived in Marseilles' . . . And he concluded with a note of false authority: 'When the time comes, I shall send you a thousand francs to provide for the most pressing demands.'

Following his wife's repeated requests, he wrote dryly: 'If in the future your letters are going to be like the ones you have been sending me ever since my arrival, I must ask you to stop. My work is not yet finished and I need to live. Bear that in mind – and stop this perpetual complaining . . . If you had the heart to understand anything other than your children, I might ask you – do you really think my life is a bed of roses?'

Two such different people, with nothing left in common, could only clash and tear each other apart. The love they both had for their children was no longer enough to bring them together again. Mette who realized that Gauguin was slipping from her did not even think of lying – she was trying to amass sufficient paintings and money to assure her children's future. From her point of view this was quite reasonable, and she made no further attempts to win back her husband.

For his part, Gauguin was prepared to provide as much as he could for the education of his children, but he felt that Mette was trying to extract the maximum from him. He thought she was earning large sums of money from the sale of his pictures, since she refused to give him details of any sales she made, and he was angry that he could not count on her help in case of fresh difficulties.

FROM RUE VERCINGETORIX TO CONCARNEAU

'The more I try, the less I succeed,' this seems to have been Paul Gauguin's motto during his last stay in Europe. He knew what he had to do, but he gave way to his impulses and upset his health and his budget. He moved to a studio at 6 rue Vercingetorix together with an extraordinary creature, whom he had found goodness only knows where. Annah, the Javanese girl, provided him with the exotic quality that he missed in the Parisian fogs. She had a skin of ebony, and he was to do a portrait of her, sitting nude in a quilted armchair. According to his friends, Gauguin had allegedly 'invited' her out of spite, when Juliette Huet had refused to come and live with him. He furnished the place somewhat freakishly, and dressed likewise. Jean de Rotonchamp has left us a detailed description of the place where for a whole season the artist led a joyful life.

A farmhouse doorway led on to a courtyard which the sculptors cluttered up with blocks of stone. At the far end was a building made of glass and light materials, bought at the time of the demolition of the Universal Exhibition of 1889. Gauguin's studio was the third and last at the end of a long veranda that ran the length of the first floor. On the panes of the front door decorated by the artist himself were the words 'Te Faruru' (Make love here). A bedroom, and a studio painted a light chrome yellow, this was Gauguin's domain. On the walls there hung his own works, and a few canvases of his friends, *Sunflowers* by Van Gogh, some drawings of Odilon Redon, a still life by Cézanne, and also some Japanese prints, and reproductions of Cranach and Botticelli, and the whole surrounded by Polynesian objects—weapons, musical instruments, and exotic shells. By way of furniture, there was a couch, a piano, and an enormous camera mounted on a tripod. In addition to this original interior design, there was a little monkey that perched on the artist's shoulder. Gauguin entertained his friends, poets and musicians, and all those who wished to come. Thursday was 'his day' for visits. Tea and alcohol were drunk. People would recite their poems, or perform their latest compositions, accompanying themselves at the piano. Gauguin himself read aloud the first chapters of *Noa Noa*.

Certain of his contemporaries who detested Gauguin, said many unpleasant things about the gatherings that were held in this studio. In spite of the décor, the atmosphere was rather formal, and it was the poets rather than the few artists around Gauguin who set the

ROSES AND STATUETTE. C. 1890 (?)
Musée des Beaux-Arts, Rheims.

tone. Without attempting to play the 'master', Gauguin found a consolation for the humiliating failure of his exhibition in the presence and conversation of these intellectuals. He tried to cut a dash, acting the role of the civilized savage. He did not depart from his eccentric ways outside his own home. He wore a blue overcoat with mother of pearl buttons, blue waistcoat embroidered in green and yellow, stone-coloured trousers, and a grey felt hat with a blue ribbon. A walking stick he had carved himself and set with a fine pearl, and white gloves completed this outfit which was reserved for paying visits and special outings.

In spite of his whims and his unreliable temper, he never lacked friends. The group consisting of Morice, Leclercq, Sérusier, Monfreid, Maufra and Schuffenecker, who had become increasingly distant, had been joined by the composer William Molard, a violinist by the name of Schneklud, whose portrait Gauguin subsequently painted, Aristide Maillol, then still a young man, Jehan Rictus, Paco Durrio, a Spanish potter, and even celebrities like Degas and Mallarmé.

Gauguin was leading the artist's life that he loved, he was held in great esteem by a small circle, he was temporarily free of money worries, and he could paint. At least, he could have done so if he had felt inspired, and if he had wanted to. But he did not paint. Of the few works dating from this period, let us mention the *Portrait of Javanese Annah*, a *Self-Portrait*, showing him in his blue attire, with an astrakhan cap on his head, the picture of his mother as a young girl, painted from a photograph, and several Tahitian works painted from memory or from drawings he had brought with him. In order to work and be creative he had to have a stimulus, he needed an atmosphere that he had not managed to create in the studio in rue Vercingetorix. He jumped at the first opportunity to leave.

In January 1894 he went to Brussels, where the Twenty Group had invited him to exhibit. He took advantage of the opportunity to visit the museums. He was extremely enthusiastic about the primitives, and Memling in particular. In his view painting had begun to deteriorate ever since it had aspired to realism. He was quite

SELF-PORTRAIT NEAR GOLGOTHA. 1896.
Museu de Arte, Sao Paolo.

prepared to defend Rubens. He judged the masterpieces of the past in the light of his own personal aesthetic and his own criteria. For him, painting which does no more than portray reality was without interest. His true mission was to give expression to a philosophy, namely symbolism.

One question remains unanswered. Being so close at hand in Brussels, did Gauguin take the opportunity of going to see his children one last time? Jean de Rotonchamp maintains he did. It

EIAHA OHIPA – DO NOT WORK. 1896.
Hermitage Museum, Leningrad.

is a possibility, and yet it is unlikely since there is no record what-
soever of this either in Gauguin's correspondence or in the Danish
archives, which have been meticulously examined by art historians.
Sickened by life and disgusted by everything, Gauguin did not then
undertake the expense of a return ticket to Copenhagen, at a time
when he was inclined to throw money out of the window. His most
recent exchanges with Mette had hardly been encouraging, and he
was afraid of getting a cold reception, or not being received at all.

With the first fine days of April he left for Brittany. This journey was something in the nature of a pilgrimage. Accompanied by Annah and the monkey, he wanted to appear before his friends cutting the figure that he himself had begun to believe in since his previous stays there. But everything had changed. La Belle Angèle and her husband had left the district. Mother Le Gloanec had abandoned the old pension for a newly built hotel. At Le Pouldu there was the same disappointment. Marie Poupée had gone to live elsewhere, in Moëlan. Gauguin temporarily accepted the hospitality of the Polish painter, Slewinsky, and then returned to Pont-Aven to Mother Le Gloanec at the Hotel des Ajoncs d'or. There he found some old acquaintances like Filiger and Moret, but the atmosphere was no longer the same ... or was it he that had changed? His bad temper and aggressiveness only increased. They came to a head in an incident that ended badly on an outing to Concarneau on 25th May 1894.

Gauguin had set out with Annah, the monkey, and a few friends, Jourdan, Armand Seguin and an Irish painter, O'Connor. As they were walking through the port, the local children who had never seen such eccentric tourists started shouting remarks that were far from flattering, and when the artists answered back, perhaps even shaking their fists at them, they threw stones at them. Seguin caught one of them and pulled his ear. It did not take long before sailors came running up, among them the father of one of the children. The incident soon turned into a brawl. Gauguin fought furiously. He recounted: 'I landed a couple of blows on a pilot who had attacked me and he went off to fetch the crew of his boat, and then I had fifteen men on top of me. I carried on fighting, holding my own, and managing quite well. Then I caught my foot in a hole, and in falling I broke my leg. As I lay on the ground, kicks rained on me, until at last I was released ...'

A doctor on the spot confirmed that he had a broken ankle, and he had to return to Pont-Aven on a cart. He was laid up for two months. In severe pain, 'dazed by the morphine', he had ample time to reflect. Europe had given him nothing but grief and suffering. Once again life in Tahiti now appeared to him like a refuge.

TE TAMARI NO ATUA
THE BIRTH OF CHRIST, THE SON OF GOD. 1896.
Bayerische Staatsgemäldesammlungen, Munich.

THE GOVERNMENT OF THE THIRD REPUBLIC IGNORES GAUGUIN

Gauguin felt disheartened and persecuted. Defeats and insults from both the public and the law appeared to be hounding him. He lost two court cases in succession. He had brought an action against his attackers in Concarneau. The judge awarded him 600 francs damages and sentenced the sailor, René Sauban, to a mere eight days' imprisonment. 'I have had to pay five hundred and seventy-five francs in medical fees, one hundred francs for the lawyer, and all the expenses involved in being ill at a hotel...' What was worse, the sailor sold his boat and, being insolvent, never paid the 600 francs.

Marie Henry refused to return the works he had left in trust with her for four years. She regarded them as compensation, and the law supported her. Gauguin felt he was being victimized. In passing, it is worth noting that the works thus inherited by the inn-keeper of Le Pouldu were sold by auction at the Hotel Drouot in Paris in 1959: one gouache went for approximately £2,600, a carved barrel for £1,500, and a bust of Meyer de Haan that Gauguin had been particularly anxious to retrieve for £7,000.

Gauguin could find some consolation in the few landscapes, showing Brittany in colours almost as vivid as those of Tahiti. Today *David's Mill* (page 185) is one of the splendours of the Musée de l'Orangerie in Paris. But misfortune was dogging his footsteps. When he finally returned to Paris, he found that Annah, who had gone back a month earlier, had walked out taking with her anything that had taken her fancy or seemed of value from the studio in the rue Vercingetorix. Gauguin's aversion to this country where he had found nothing but meanness and wickedness was continually growing. From Pont-Aven he had already written:

'All these successive misfortunes, together with the difficulty of earning a regular income, despite my reputation, and in addition my own taste for the exotic, have led me to this irreversible decision, namely:

'In December I shall return, and do all I can to sell everything in my possession, either "en block" (sic) or piece by piece. Once I have the money in my pocket, I shall set off for the South Seas again, this time together with two friends from here, Sérusier and an Irishman. There is no point in trying to dissuade me. Nothing will stop me from leaving, and this time it will be for good.' He called all his friends to witness. To Daniel de Monfreid he stated quite definitely: 'If I am successful, I shall leave immediately in February. Then I can end my days in freedom and tranquility, without care for tomorrow, and without the eternal battle against Imbeciles . . . Painting farewell, if it is only a diversion – my own house will be made of carved wood.'

The attitude of the authorities did nothing to deter him from his decision. He had been to see the Director of Fine Arts immediately on his return from Tahiti, to settle the purchase of his pictures, which had been promised him when he left. A high-ranking official politely dismissed him. Some time later he offered one of his master works, *Ia orana Maria*, as a gift to the Luxembourg museum, but the bequest was not accepted. Before leaving he again approached Monsieur Roujon to grant him an official mission, as before, to help him in his dealings with the local authorities, but it was refused.

Charles Morice summed up the situation in an article in *Le Soir:* 'Paul Gauguin is not fortunate in his countrymen. Those among them, who for years now have been amazed at his choice to live in splendid exile in Tahiti, working in peace and in sunshine, need only look to their own ingratitude towards a man, whose work and whose name must be counted amongst the richest of our possessions, in order to find the reasons for his departure . . .'

THE SECOND AND DISASTROUS SALE

In order to sell off the canvases that had accumulated in the studio in the rue Vercingetorix, and procure the necessary capital for going into exile, Gauguin was relying on a big sale at the Hotel Drouot. The catalogue published for the occasion provides us with precious information today. The list consisted of forty-nine paintings, drawings and engravings–those paintings from the Durand-Ruel exhibition that had not been sold plus several others which he considered worthy of being included.

It was not Octave Mirbeau who was asked to write the preface, but August Strindberg, who had attended Gauguin's 'Thursdays' on several occasions. The Swedish writer, whose expressive and symbolist style in his novels and dramas appealed to Gauguin, replied in a long letter, which gives an insight into the reactions of a cultured man in the year 1895.

'You are quite determined to have the preface to your catalogue written by me, in memory of the winter of 1894–95 we have spent here, behind the Institute, not far from the Pantheon, and above all close to the cemetery of Montparnasse.

TE RERIOA — THE DREAM. 1897.
Courtauld Institute, London.

'I should have willingly given you this souvenir to take away with you to this South Sea Island, where you are going in search of space and a setting in harmony with your own powerful stature, but from the beginning I have felt that I was in an ambiguous situation, and I am replying right away to your request by saying "I cannot" or more brutishly "I do not want to".

'At the same time, I owe you an explanation for my refusal...' Strindberg was writing a history of painting since 1876, and he ended it with a description of an evening spent in the studio in rue Vercingetorix.

'I saw on your walls this confusion of sunlit paintings that haunted me in my sleep that night. I saw trees that no botanist would ever find, animals that Cuvier never dreamed of, and people that you alone could have created.

'A sea that looked as if it had flowed from a volcano, and a sky that no God could inhabit. – Monsieur, I said in my dream, you have created a new earth and a new sky, but I do not feel at ease in your creation. For me it is too ablaze with sunlight, I who prefer chiaroscuro. And your paradise is inhabited by an Eve who is not my ideal, for believe it or not I really do have an ideal or two of womanhood!

'. . . No, Gauguin has not been formed out of the rib of Chavannes, nor from that of Manet or Bastien – Lepage.

'What then is he? He is Gauguin, the savage who hates the restrictions of civilization, some kind of Titan, who jealous of the Creator, in his lost moments produces his own small version of the creation, he is the child that takes his toys to pieces in order to make new ones, he rejects and defies, preferring to see the sky as red instead of blue like the masses.'

'Upon my word, it seems that as I have been getting heated writing this, I am beginning to have a certain understanding for the art of Gauguin!

NEVERMORE O TAITI. 1897.
Courtauld Institute, London.

'A modern author has been criticized for not painting real figures, but *just simply* creating his characters himself. *Just simply!*

'Bon voyage, Master! Only, do come back and see me. I might then perhaps learn to understand your Art better, which would enable me to write a real preface to a new catalogue in a new Hotel Drouot, for I am also beginning to feel a tremendous need to turn primitive and create a new world.'

Gauguin appreciated this letter, for he immediately decided to publish it by way of a preface. He thanked Strindberg for it by return of post, and since he was writing to a man of letters he paid special attention to his style in order to justify – paradoxically – the unpolished style he adopted in his painting.

'I received your letter today; your letter, which is a preface for my catalogue. I decided to ask you for this preface when I saw you the other day in my studio, playing the guitar and singing; your blue northern eyes were closely examining the pictures hanging on the walls. I could sense that you recoiled – this was a clash between your civilization and my own barbarism.

'Civilization makes you suffer. Barbarism for me is a form of rejuvenation.

'Standing in front of the Eve of my choice, whom I have painted in the forms and harmonies of another world, your own memories perhaps returned to an unhappy past. The Eve of your civilized conception turns you and nearly always turns us all into woman-haters. The primeval Eve, who made you afraid in my studio, might one day smile less bitterly upon you. This world, which perhaps no Cuvier and no botanist could find, might be a Paradise, which I alone have sketched out. And it is a far cry from the rough sketch to the realization of the dream. What does it matter? To catch a glimpse of happiness, is this not a foretaste of nirvana?

'The Eve I have painted (and she alone) can remain naked before our eyes. In this state ours could not walk without shame and possibly being too beautiful she might arouse evil and suffering.

'In order to make you understand my train of thought, let me make a comparison, not directly between these two women, but between the Maori or Turanian tongue spoken by my Eve and the language spoken by the woman you have chosen from all others, an inflected, European language.

'In the Oceanic languages, the essential elements have been preserved in all their crudity, and isolated or joined without any care for politeness, everything is stark, vivid and primordial.

'Whereas in inflected languages, the roots by which they, like all languages, began, disappear in daily use. They are like a splendid mosaic that one admires without noticing the more or less clumsy way in which the stones have been joined. Only a practised eye will detect the process of construction.

'Excuse this long philological digression; I felt it necessary to explain the primitive technique I had to use in order to portray a Turanian land and people.

'It remains for me, dear Strindberg, to thank you.'

Collectors in 1895 were, however, not receptive to this dialogue. In order to maintain respectable prices, Gauguin was forced into buying back the majority of the pictures put up for sale, and had to pay the legal taxes on these fictitious sales.

However, on 18th February 1895 numerous friends of Gauguin were present in Room 7 of the Hotel Drouot, and the majority of them bought at least one of his works. Right at the beginning Degas bought the *Woman with Mangoes* (1893) for 450 francs, and later Manet's *Olympia* for 230 francs. Schuffenecker himself, the disgruntled friend, who did not hesitate to criticize Gauguin publicly, went away with several works, admittedly at low prices. According to the record of the sale, the total proceeds came to 3,000 francs, of which Gauguin was left with almost 2,000 francs. This was nothing like the 9,600 francs from the 1891 sale!

Though short of capital, Gauguin left rich in promises. The proprietor of the Café des Variétés was going to pay him 2,600 francs for six pictures. A dealer named Talboum owed him 800 francs for one canvas, and the picture-framer, Dosbourg, also owed him 600 francs. Finally, two dealers, Levy and Chaudet assured him that they would, sooner or later sell enough for him to live on.

NAVE NAVE MAHANA – DELIGHTFUL DAYS. 1896.
Musée des Beaux-Arts, Lyons.

Gauguin left from Marseilles on 29th June on the 'Oceanie', on which he had already travelled once before as far as New Zealand. He did not inform his wife, and kept his friends, who wanted to make a farewell gesture of their affection, from coming to the station, pleading as excuse his sensitivity and dread of emotional demonstration. This time he knew the kind of life that awaited him and he had chosen it himself. He had retained his capacity for enthusiasm, but he parted feeling spiritually and mortally wounded. The attitude of his wife and of the Parisian art connoisseurs had turned him into a confirmed misanthrope, persecuted, an enemy of civilization, of its hypocrisies and its treacherous cruelties. Later he wrote: 'See what I have done with marriage – I have gone off without a word. Let my family manage how they can on their own, for if I am the only one to help them ..! Yes, indeed, I am a real criminal. Who cares! Michelangelo was the same, and I am no Michelangelo.'

His physical stamina was also not what it had been. The fracture in his leg had given him a lot of pain, and he had caught syphilis from a prostitute whom he had met in a dance hall in Avenue du Maine. His friends had already recognized the first symptoms of the disease around the ankle wound.

What then could have been the frame of mind of this man, leaving for the Pacific Isles without any hope of return? He believed himself to be courageous, rational and determined. In reality, this decision satisfied a spontaneous impulse–he fled from civilization, from France, because it rejected him, and he was unappreciated and scorned there. In going in search of the primitive life, that he would have liked to regard as ideal, but which at least provided him with the inspiration and the energy to work and women who were not merely favourite models, he was relinquishing a universe in which life would have suited him perfectly well, had he not lacked money.

THE JOYS OF LIFE IN PUNAUIA

As on his first visit, Gauguin found the island and its inhabitants delightful. He was surprised at the changes that had taken place during his absence: 'Papeete, the capital of this Eden of Tahiti, is now lit by electricity. The large lawn in front of the old King's Palace is now ruined by a merry-go-round . . .'

All that we know of the last eight years of Gauguin's life from 1895 to 1903 comes from administrative records and letters to his friends, and to Daniel de Monfreid in particular, in which he only wrote what he wanted known. This correspondence enables us to relive this magnificent and tragic period of Gauguin's existence.

He rented a plot of ground on the sea shore, at Punauia, half-way between Papeete and Mataiea, where he had lived in 1892 and 1893. He did not wish to return there because Tehura was now married–

TE ARII VAHINE – WOMAN WITH MANGOES. 1896.
Private Collection.

she bestowed her favours on Gauguin, but did not wish to leave her
husband and her children. Gauguin had a large native dwelling built
by the side of the road, on a shaded site, overlooked by the mountain. It was divided into two parts, a bedroom, which was dark and
cool, and a studio with light coming through the roof. 'On the floor,
rush matting and my old Persian carpet–the whole is decorated by
drapery, knick-knacks, and drawings.' He led a joyful life: 'Night
after night there are wild young girls in my bed . . .'

EVE AND THE SERPENT. 1896.
Ny Carlsberg Glyptothek, Copenhagen.

Behind this hut was a lean-to where he kept his horse and carriage which he harnessed for drives and for his trips to Papeete. He was still nursing his weak ankle. He lived comfortably without worrying about saving. He kept accounts, and by adding up all that various friends and Parisian dealers owed him, he arrived at a total of 4,500 francs–enough to live on for two years. Alas, by December he had still received nothing. The vicious circle began anew, and he began to get into debt. The privations he endured weakened him, and the wound in his leg began to trouble him again. He begged Daniel de Monfreid to press all his debtors. He could not believe that he had been forgotten in such a short time, nor that they were taking advantage of his absence in order not to pay him. That winter of 1895–96 was a severe ordeal.

From April onwards his latest Tahitian girl, Pahura, aged thirteen and a half, inspired him and posed for him. The work stimulated him and raised his morale. He spoke warmly of *Te Arri Vahine* (first called 'The King's Wife', today in the Pushkin Museum) (page 196): 'I have just done a canvas 1 metre 30 by 1 metre, which I believe is better than anything that has gone before–a nude queen lying on a green carpet, with a servant gathering fruit, and two old men near some large trees discussing the tree of knowledge; in the background is the water's edge... I think that in terms of colour, I have never done anything of such a great and sober harmony. The trees are in blossom, the dog is on guard, and the two doves on the right are cooing...' But his life was a succession of ups and downs. Whatever the value and interest of his work, from now on he doubted that he would ever see his talent recognized. 'What is the use of sending this canvas, when there are so many others which do not get sold and only make people howl. This one will make them howl even more. I am condemned to die of good will, if I am not to die of starvation...'

While waiting for mail from Europe, which might bring him a money order, Gauguin borrowed and reflected. He devised a system which would guarantee his own maintenance, and would at the same time benefit those art collectors who had confidence in him. Daniel

VAÏRUMATI. 1897.
Louvre, Paris.

de Monfreid was to get fifteen of them to agree to this scheme, and his future would be secure. In order to pay him 2,400 francs a year, each person needed only to subscribe 160 francs, a small sum. In exchange Gauguin undertook to send fifteen good canvases, which they could share amongst themselves either by agreement or by drawing lots. And he enclosed a list of names with his letter. He also suggested that Daniel de Monfreid should approach the Comte de la Rochefoucault, who was already paying a pension of 1,200 francs to Bernard and to Filiger, and sent him nine canvases in the care of an officer on the despatch vessel 'La Durance'.

He received 200 francs from the Comte de la Rochefoucault and 200 from a friend of Schuffenecker. The latter had also circulated a petition for the State to come to Gauguin's aid. Puvis de Chavannes, Degas, Mallarmé, Mirbeau, Arsène Alexandre and Roger-Marx had already signed it. For his part, Morice tried approaching Roujon, the Minister for Fine Arts, who refused to buy anything by Gauguin, but also sent him 200 francs. Gauguin was furious, and sent the money back to Roujon. As for the others, he was indignant that they had not thought of buying a picture from him instead of sending him charity, which desperate circumstances obliged him to accept. 'I am very weak, and I have nothing but water to drink and a little rice cooked in water to eat in order to restore my strength.' The condition of his leg had deteriorated to such an extent that he had to go into the hospital at Papeete during the summer, and he was unable to meet the cost of his stay there. By the end of the year Chaudet had still only sent him 200 francs. Gauguin was now prepared to sacrifice everything in order to survive: 'my precarious situation grows more and more intolerable. I am tired of saying that this is no time to haggle over prices, sell all the pictures that belong to me at any price.'

His stay in hospital had restored his strength somewhat, and he now began to spend his time on sculpture. His sculptures were, he said, all in the garden – a lion, a woman, a nude which had earned him the censure of the priest.

In this year his paintings were illuminated by a reddish flame-like glow; the figures were bathed in an unnatural light, and existed in a sort of earthly paradise, as in *Nave Nave Mahana* (page 212). Was he going through a spell of mysticism, a period of respite, in which he felt drawn towards meditation? Was it the birth of another child that had caused him to regard the future with greater serenity? He declared, not without cynicism: 'Oh, if only I had my due, my life would be extraordinarily calm and happy. I shall soon be the father of a half-caste.' This bantering tone contrasts sharply with his actual feelings. There are two moving canvases that date from this time. One is entitled *The Baby* (page 197), showing a Tahitian girl seated on a wooden bench with a newly-born child on her lap. On the right, a Maori angel hovers as if in annunciation, while in the stable in the background, among the resting cattle and pigs, there appears lying on the ground the figure of Christ, a halo around his head and bathed in a mystical light. Gauguin mingles the purity of the divine with a tenderness that is altogether human. This was not the only time he placed religious themes in a Tahitian setting. *The Last Supper* (page 189) was also set in a typical native dwelling, and achieved the same effect by a harmonisation of the supernatural and the concrete.

In another picture, a young native girl in the abandoned posture of a woman after childbirth, lies sharply outlined against a yellow bedspread, a cat curled up at her feet (page 205). It is the setting that gives the work its significance – once again there is a stable with cattle, and the child held by a Tahitian woman has a halo.

Like Tehura, Gauguin was mingling Christianity with local customs. But whether their inspiration was Christian or purely Tahitian, his paintings now took on increasingly religious significance. In them he admitted his preoccupation with survival in another world or in other beings. This duality did not trouble him in the least, and he synthesized it in his painting, even painting himself once again as Christ in his *Self-Portrait near Golgotha* (page 202). The emaciated face, bordered by the hair and the beard, bears an enigmatic expression. The pale and luminous tunic draws the attention towards the gaze that seems to come from afar and looks beyond us all. This dramatic and intentionally disquieting face tells us perhaps more of the sufferings endured by the artist than all the long enumerations of debts that fill his correspondence. Such is the power of painting that it can portray horrifying reality in an almost tangible way, instead of by prosaically narrating facts.

ATTEMPT AT SUICIDE

1897 was to be an even worse year for Gauguin than the one that had just gone by. However it began more auspiciously, for in January

THE WHITE HORSE. 1898.
Louvre, Paris.

TAHITI. 1897.
John C. Savoir Collection.

he received 1,200 francs from Chaudet, followed by 1,035 francs. Immediately he decided to get himself admitted to hospital again. He instructed Daniel de Monfreid to send him 'about fifty assorted brushes . . .' The colours he asked for give us some idea of his palette: ten tubes of ultramarine, five cobalt, fifteen carmine, five rose madder, twenty white, ten yellow ochre, five brown ochre, five emerald, three light vermilion, two cadmium yellow no. 2, and three cadmium lemon, and he added: 'What a lot of requests, my poor

Daniel, I put you to such trouble and work. Also, take something as an advance towards the cost of frames, etc. . . . and of course for the expense you have on my account.'

But the Europeans meanwhile were becoming more and more insulting towards him. His fellow countrymen no long concealed their contempt for this artist who was living like the natives. At the hospital they wanted to put him in the native ward, but he refused.

Gauguin now became increasingly bitter and aggressive. He was severely critical of all the negligence and irregularities in the administration. He attacked the postal service for the delays in the handling of mail. After the failure of a military expedition, supported by the cruiser 'Duguay-Trouin', he sent Charles Morice a detailed account of the affair, advising him to publish it in a virulent article in the metropolitan press.

At the same time he pleaded for silence about his work: 'I tell you that I am no great believer in exhibitions. That imbecile, Schuff, does nothing but dream of exhibitions, publicity, etc. . . . and does not see that these have a disastrous effect. I have many enemies, and always shall have, perhaps more and more as time goes on; each time I exhibit they wake up, and disgust and keep away the true lovers of art. The best way to sell is still silence.'

He sent some of his recent canvases to Monfreid, putting them in the care of Dr Gouzer, ship's doctor on the 'Duguay-Trouin'. Among these was *Te Rerioa–The Dream* (page 208). 'Everything in this canvas is a dream; whether it is the child, or the mother, or the man on horseback riding along the path, or maybe it's just the dream of the painter!!!' Another dramatically dark canvas takes up the theme of *Manao Tupapau* once again–a woman is lying stretched out, brooding, with an apprehensive look on her face. Behind her, outside the house two apostle-like figures are talking. On one wall there is a raven, bird of ill omen, and in a corner the word of Edgar Allan Poe: *Nevermore* (page 209).

'I wanted,' he said, 'with a simple nude to suggest a certain barbaric luxury of former times. The whole picture consists of a blending of deliberately subdued and mournful colours; it is neither the silk, nor the velvet, nor the cambric, nor the gold that produce this luxury, but the substance enriched by the hand of the artist. No nonsense . . . It is man's imagination alone that has enriched this dwelling with his own fantasy.

'As for the title, it is not Edgar Poe's raven, it is the devil's bird, on the look-out . . .' Indeed, the whole expresses the menace of a fate that is as inevitable as it is incomprehensible.

Almost as if he had foreseen them, fresh misfortunes overtook Gauguin. Just as he was enjoying living peacefully for a few months, a brief note from Mette informed him that their daughter Aline had died suddenly of pneumonia. Gauguin confessed to his friend Daniel the strange way in which grief had affected him. At first he had been amazed to feel nothing, not the slightest inclination to weep; he imagined that his sufferings had made him insensitive. But suddenly he felt a great emptiness spreading through him, followed by a fit of dull rage. He succumbed to a deep depression, and for several weeks he only came out of his torpor to abuse the heavens: 'the feeling I had was one of anger and fury, in some ways like the delirium of a patient who is being tortured and yet craves for fresh suffering. Since my childhood misfortune has pursued me. Never any luck, never any joy. Everything always against me until I cry out: "My God, if you exist, I accuse you of injustice and evil." Yes, at the news of poor Aline's death, I doubted everything, and laughed in defiance. What is the use of virtue, hard work, and intelligence?'

It was not until a few months later that he wrote Mette a last letter, curiously phrased, and without any address or date:

'I am reading over the shoulder of a friend who writes:

Madame,

I asked you that on 7th June, my birthday, the children should write to me simply "My dear Papa" and a signature. And you replied: "You have no money, don't count on it."

'I shall not say "May God keep you" but more realistically "may your conscience slumber peacefully to spare you waiting for death as a form of delivery".

Your husband.

'And this same friend writes to me: "I have just lost my daughter, I no longer love God. Like my mother, she was called Aline. Everyone loves in their own way – for some love is extolled to the tomb, for others . . . Her grave over there and those flowers, mere illusion. Her grave is here by my side; my tears are its flowers." '

He was so deeply upset that when his son, Clovis, died three years later in 1900, his friends refrained from informing him of it.

WHERE DO WE COME FROM, WHAT ARE WE, WHERE ARE WE GOING. 1897.
Museum of Fine Art, Boston, U.S.A.

After the death of Aline, Gauguin's psychological make-up became more complicated. He was no longer simply a rebel and an outcast, an outlaw devoted to a superior morality, dreaming of the ultimate rule of justice; admixed in his behaviour now was an unconscious form of masochism. He rebelled against the blows dealt him by fate and men, and yet this battling spirit was mitigated by a confused satisfaction. In so far as everything was conspiring against him, he experienced a sort of unhealthy pleasure, as if the very unanimity of the forces lined up against him proved that he alone stood for the truth. Meanwhile every kind of set-back befell him.

BREASTS WITH RED FLOWERS. 1899.
Metropolitan Museum of Art, New York.

When the owner of the piece of land where he had built his house died, the land was sold and Gauguin evicted. He was obliged to demolish what he had erected with such love and compelled to find another place to rebuild his home. With the greatest difficulty he secured a loan for 1,000 francs from the Agricultural Bank of Tahiti and bought a plot of land for 700 francs. The proofs he had to furnish were a terrible humiliation for him. Moreover this debt was to hang around his neck like a millstone for several years, and become an obsession with him.

The move was not entirely without compensations; he had acquired a plantation of a hundred coconut palms which he hoped to cultivate, and he even thought of planting vanilla, and had already calculated this would bring in a yield of 50 francs a year. Needless to say, nothing ever came of this.

He was continually troubled by ill-health. For several months his letters were few and brief; he developed conjunctivitis 'and for two days now they have been cauterising the granulations with copper sulphate. I am very much afraid that I shall never be fully restored to health'. It was not only his eyes that were troubling him; he suffered from spells of giddiness and attacks of fever, and sometimes he would be unable to get up for several days. His insufficient diet prevented him from overcoming his depression. It made him desperate that he could not manage to sell enough paintings to bring in 2,500 francs a year, while his juniors, people like Maurice Denis, were already earning 10,000 francs at least.

He was concerned about the reactions his paintings produced, and the slightest word of praise from Daniel de Monfreid was enough to restore some of his will to live . . . 'You have admired them; good, for in my present state, I cannot really judge their true value. You reproach me for not taking enough care over my materials. Oh, but I do pay just as much attention to them as to the painting – but the preparation of the materials leaves much to be desired. This is perfectly true. But what did you expect of me in the state I was in, so nervous and impatient, that preparation worried me and made me tired. Then, after all, the paintings you mentioned were rolled up by a naval officer – I was in hospital at the time – who did not know how it should be done, and they stayed rolled up like this for two whole months without air and in extreme heat, anything could have happened to them.' He then gave very precise technical instructions on how they should be restored. When one thinks of the travelling and general conditions to which the works of Gauguin's Tahitian period were subjected, one cannot help but marvel at their present freshness and state of preservation.

Art alone, however, was not enough to make Gauguin hold on to life. Without news from France, except from his one friend, without means of support, without any hope of paying off his debt, and with his body tormented with sickness, he gave up struggling, and decided to allow himself to die. From September onwards, the same theme runs through all his letters: 'Without a dealer, without anyone to supply me with my daily bread, what is to become of me? I can see no way out, except Death which brings absolute deliverance . . .' He even gave up painting. 'For three months I have not touched a brush, the colours you sent me will now be useless, and nobody here would exchange them for twopence worth of bread; that's the bitter irony of it.'

'Today my decision to put an end to it all has changed, in the sense that nature is taking a hand in it, but it will take a long time . . .' Gauguin summed up: 'I believe that everything that should and should not have been said, has already been said about me. All I want now is silence, silence and more silence. Let me die in peace, forgotten . . .'

In a postscript to the same letter, he asked Monfreid, should he disappear, to keep all the canvases that had been left with him for himself. 'My family has more than enough.'

He received the issue of the *Revue Blanche* containing the first instalment of *Noa Noa*, but its publication seemed 'inopportune' to him, and what was worse he had not been paid for it. Doubtless Charles Morice had once again been in need of this money. Gauguin was surprised, but not indignant any more. He merely issued express instructions that his wife should not get a penny of it!

THE CRUCIFIXION.
Dr Paressant Collection, Nantes.

STILL LIFE WITH MANGOES. 1896 (?)
Private Collection.

From letter to letter we follow the dramatic development of the idea of suicide, then suddenly there is a long silence. Gauguin had made a bet with himself; if he did not receive anything by the mail that arrived in January 1898, he would kill himself. In December his mind was made up, but he did not want to disappear without leaving anything behind him. He set to work on a big composition that he had been thinking about for a long time. He was to work on it night and day for weeks, and it was to be the masterpiece *Where do we come from, what are we, where are we going* (page 224).

He painted like one possessed, very rapidly and without a stop, but he exercised such mastery over his subject that it would hardly have been credible, if he had not admitted it himself: 'Why, this is no canvas painted like a Puvis de Chavannes, with studies from nature and a portfolio of preparatory sketches, etc. ... All this is painted without any model, straight off the brush, on sacking canvas full of knots and wrinkles, thus the general appearance is extremely rough . . .'

It was to be his pictorial testament, the sum of all his ideas, his feelings and his agonies. At the same time it presented a fundamental question that remained eternally unanswered and contained a philosophy of life. 'I sought to put into it all my energy before dying, such a painful emotion under terrible circumstances, and such a clear vision, without any alterations, that the feeling of hastiness disappeared and it suddenly came alive. It does not smack of models, professionalism, and obedience to rules – things I have always tried to avoid, though with some apprehension.'

The painting is 3 metres 75 by 1 metre 39, and Gauguin described it at great length. His own analysis provides us with a key to its symbolism. It was conceived in decorative terms: 'The two upper corners are chrome yellow with the inscription on the left hand and my signature on the right, like a fresco with damaged corners on a gold wall.' The striking thing is, that in following the author's explanations, the painting does not read from left to right in the western way, but from right to left, from birth to death. 'On the right at the bottom there is a sleeping baby, and then three squatting women. Two figures dressed in purple are exchanging thoughts; a crouching figure deliberately enormous despite the perspective, raises its arms in the air and looks astonished at these two figures who dare to think of their destiny.'

Gauguin had had the opportunity to mediate on human destiny at the birth of his last child, the little half-caste daughter of Pahura. This forms the first part of this composition, that is very clearly divided into three equal parts, and linked by the continous melody of the landscape which forms the background.

'A figure in the centre is picking a fruit. Two cats by a child. A white goat. The idol with both arms mysteriously and rhythmically raised seems to be pointing out the beyond.' This idol has already appeared in other pictures by Gauguin and separates the two left-hand thirds of the composition, maturity and old age. 'The fruit-picking symbolizes the pleasures of life, the harvests, and fertility. The fullness of the figure is explicit. It would be happiness unmarred were it not for the presence of the idol constituting a reminder of eternal truths, a menace forever threatening humanity.'

Gauguin continues the enumeration of the figures in this strange fresco: 'A squatting figure seems to be listening to the idol; then, finally, an old woman close to death seems to accept and be resigned to her own thoughts, bringing the story to a close; at her feet is a strange white bird, holding a lizard between its feet, representing the uselessness of empty words.'

In fact the squatting Tahitian woman seems to be listening to the old woman rather than to the idol. She appeared in an earlier canvas of 1897, *Vaïrumati* (page 217), as did the white bird holding the lizard. This symbol of the bird seems to be a more complex development of the raven in *Nevermore*. An analysis of this work by Georges Wildenstein, which appeared in the *Gazette des Beaux Arts* in 1958, shows that in this great composition Gauguin used numerous elements that had appeared in his earlier works. This explains how he had been able to complete a composition of this importance so rapidly and how he had been able to dispense with models. He had already worked out each of the figures previously.

The landscape forms a musical accompaniment to the melancholy meditation of the figures. 'The whole takes place by the side of a stream in a wood. In the background is the sea, and then the mountains of the neighbouring island. Despite the changing tones, the aspect of the landscape from one end to the other is of a constant Veronese blue and green.' These cold and dull colours reflect the melancholy of the general theme and bring out the brilliant colour of the skin. 'Against this all the nudes stand out in brilliant orange.' In this way the contrast between life and death is brought out in material form.

The inspiration for this masterpiece arose out of a study Gauguin had made, and pompously entitled *The Catholic Church and Modern Times*. In this he drew a parallel between the beliefs of different people. He confused religions, asserting his own faith and criticizing

Christianity, which he regarded as 'idolatry'. His solitude was conducive to reflections of a decidedly confused kind, from which there emerged only one clear idea, that our world is incomprehensible. 'The unfathomable mystery remains, that it has been, still is, and always will be unfathomable. God does not belong to the scholar or to the logician, he belongs to poets, to the Dream. He is the symbol of Beauty, of Beauty personified.' Such is the profound lesson of *Where do we come from, what are we, where are we going.*

FAA IHEIHE — PREPARATIONS FOR A FESTIVAL. 1898.
Tate Gallery, London.

Gauguin had come all this way, endured much hardship, and passed so many sleepless nights in order to recognize the powerlessness of man and intellect, and to bow to the mystery of life and of the world. An irrational and romantic attitude that contrasted with his desire to find an explanation for everything. He was now physically and mentally at the end of his strength. He had synthesized this last idea into a great work of which he was proud. All that now remained for him was to die.

He fled to the mountains, taking with him a strong dose of arsenic with which he had been treating his eczema (or syphilis). He looked for a lonely and deserted spot, took the poison and waited for death. In his eagerness to die, he had taken such a strong dose that it made him vomit. The whole night he was in agonising pain, and at dawn he made his way back to the village, exhausted, terribly ill, and took to his bed. It took him weeks to regain his strength. This fresh ordeal had weakened him even further. The small amount of money he had just received from his dealer, Chaudet, and from Daniel de Monfreid enabled him to nurse himself. But in May the settlement of his debt to the Agricultural Bank of Tahiti fell due.

GAUGUIN THE OFFICIAL AND POLEMIST

Gauguin had not yet reached the end of his Calvary. The years of 1898, 1899 and 1900 were still to come. He lived through them, rebelling, and sometimes complaining, but he never resigned himself to leaving, and rejected all thought of returning to France. At one time he almost gave in to Daniel de Monfreid, but this same friend later advised him against coming back for fear of compromising the interest that was now being shown in his work and spoiling the legend, which after so much sacrifice was finally being credited.

As his strength returned after his attempt at suicide, he became temporarily optimistic and was inspired to paint a new composition of large dimensions. He had been reading Telemachus, and discovered a similarity between ancient Greece and Tahiti. *Faa Iheihe – Preparations for a Festival* (page 232) develops this parallel. Here Gauguin was no longer depicting human beings burdened down by fate, these were demi-gods promenading in a garden of Eden. The trees form unreal arabesques, and the beings and objects are bathed in a divine light. Even more striking than this profound and radical change, as evident in the study mentioned above, is the difference in the rhythm of the composition and in the execution of the figures. *Where do we come from* is all curves; the figures are for the most part either seated or stretched out on the ground, the curving arabesques following the undulations of the earth; in *Faa Iheihe* everything is treated in vertical terms, expressing elevation, *élan* and natural ease. The general effect is one of serenity and a detachment from material contingencies that mark a new period in the work of Gauguin. His unsuccessful attempt at suicide had no effect in terms of style. The painter remain-

OVIRI (THE SAVAGE). SELF-PORTRAIT. C. 1893.
Private Collection.

ed faithful to his technique that was at once supple and nervous, and he retained his habit of covering every shape with pigment without saturating it, often allowing the coating and the weave of the canvas to show through.

This detachment and euphoric calm are evident in all the subsequent canvases of Gauguin, and he never returned to the tragic forms from before *Where do we come from*. This is to be seen in *Breasts with Red Flowers* (page 225) as well as in the enigmatic

RAVE TE HITI RAMU – THE IDOL. 1898.
Hermitage Museum, Leningrad.

monster, half-man, half-statue in *Rave te hiti ramu* (see above), to name only the most famous of these later pictures.

This indifference, which temporarily made Gauguin cease to rebel, led him to accept a post as employee in the Public Works of Tahiti. He did surveys of land, and worked on plans and other tasks where his knowledge of drawing enabled him to carry out his duties without any great distinction. He no longer painted. He had managed with great difficulty to secure a postponement of the loan from the Agri-

235

cultural Bank by mortgaging his property at Punauia. He was saving, for he did not wish to leave his post and start painting again until he had accumulated a sum of money that would free him of all financial worry. With the money he received he settled his debts. He dispatched *Where do we come from* to Monfreid through a naval officer, and a money order for about a 1,000 francs liberated Gauguin from his drudgery in the surveying department.

Meanwhile the dealer Vollard now entered Gauguin's life discreetly, as was his fashion. Vollard's life reads like a novel, mingling at times with the history of contemporary painting. Initially a second-hand bookseller and stamp dealer, he was then employed by a very conventional gallery, before setting up on his own and dealing in drawings and prints by Willette, Steinlein and Forain. Since 1893 he had a shop in rue Lafitte and became Cézanne's dealer.

Vollard's tactics were to feign indifference! He pretended to be asleep – this was a business trick for which he became famous. It gave him a double advantage: artists would think he found their prices too high and would drop them without waiting for him to stir himself to reply; buyers on the other hand would raise their offers. Gauguin had always detested and distrusted him profoundly. Being of a fiery nature himself, with a quick reply ever on the tip of his tongue, he could not abide the affected nonchalance of this wily businessman.

Vollard, however, came to an agreement with Daniel de Monfreid and exhibited a collection of Gauguin's latest paintings in his gallery from 17th November to 8th December 1898. He bought a parcel of paintings in advance at a competitive price, and later repeated this operation. Daniel de Monfreid had agreed, because this lump sum came to a substantial amount which might help Gauguin out of difficulty, and after all, this was what Gauguin had been urging him to do. But in this case he had gone too far. Gauguin had no confidence in the dealer and complained bitterly that a large section of his most recent work was now in the hands of Vollard. There was now no hope of selling anything to his private collectors for at least another year. Nine canvases for 1,000 francs – an average of 110 francs

TE AVAE NO MARIA — THE MONTH OF MARY. 1899.
Hermitage Museum, Leningrad.

for each! 'This man is shameless, ready to exploit poverty for a few meagre cents, and next time, encouraged by his success, he will offer you half the price.'

The exhibition caused a certain stir, the press took notice of it, and André Fontainas published a critical study in the *Mercure de France*, to which Gauguin replied in a long letter, in which he set out his own conceptions.

Gauguin seized upon everything as an excuse to argue, dispute and battle for the truth he believed in. This was not restricted to art. He became increasingly irritable towards affairs of everyday life in Tahiti. No doubt this was owing to the solitary existence he had led for so long. He did not mix with any of the colonial officials, but spent his time daydreaming, and even began to imagine he was seeing things. He was to complain to the attorney that he had seen a native sweeping the thickets on his land with an indoor broom. Gauguin wanted to bring an action for violation of the privacy of his home and for attempted theft, and the attorney had great difficulty in dissuading him from doing so.

Gauguin continued to be enraged and disturbed. He felt persecuted, and imagined his mail was being stolen, and attacked the legal representatives. His disputes with the officers of the law created such a stir that in June 1899 a Tahiti newspaper, *Les Guêpes* (The Wasps) opened its columns to him, in the hope of exploiting his polemics towards political ends.

Gauguin fell for the ruse; he poured out invective, expressed his indignation, and did not hesitate to use the most violent and offensive language, regardless of the fact that he could be prosecuted for defamation. With the journalist's pen in his hand, he recalled that he was the grandson of Flora Tristan. Just as she had fought against the exploitation of the proletariat, he in his turn hoped to put an end to the excesses and injustices of colonial power. He took up the pettiest causes that were pointed out to him, and became a poisonous reporter of all the gossip of Papeete, introducing the religious conflicts between the Protestant and Catholic schools into his diatribes. He even hoped to provoke the attorney, Charlier, to a duel. The more the latter persisted in ignoring his attacks, the more furious Gauguin became. He even composed his own defence speech in advance for his subsequent trial for defamation, although when the time came he did not use it. Gauguin was at the height of a schizoid attack—he ignored reality and was ready to exploit everything as fuel for his anger. The columns of *Les Guêpes* were now too restricted for his passion for writing, and from August 1899 he published his own news-sheet under the name of *Le Sourire, journal sérieux* (The Smile, a serious newspaper). He used to print about thirty copies by 'limeograph' based on the Edison system, a very primitive form of cyclostyle. There were to be nine issues, the last appearing in April 1900.

Today these writings have lost their topicality. In them Gauguin launched into futile battles, and in so doing neglected his painting. But the collected issues of *Le Sourire* are interesting for the symbolist or satirical drawings with which Gauguin decorated most of them. These drawings have a primitive vigour that is even more stylized than the woodcuts of *Noa Noa*.

The year 1899 came to an end with Gauguin continuing his press campaign, and ceaselessly trying to raise more money on credit. He was also trying to find a better method of varnishing his canvases, which would prevent them from cracking on the long sea journey back to France. Daniel had just had a daughter, and Gauguin another child, which was almost white. The birth of these children forged yet another link between the two men. However, Chaudet, the last dealer to remain faithful to the artist, did not reply to his requests, and Gauguin was once again without money. His painting suffered from his precarious financial situation. 'You say: why don't you paint more thickly, so as to create a surface of a richer substance? I don't disagree, and indeed at times I should very much like to; but I am finding it increasingly impossible, since I have to take the cost of the colours into account. I have very little left, although I have been using them sparingly, and I cannot ask you for more, until I know that I can be certain that my material future is assured. If you could find me someone who would undertake to pay me 2,400 francs a year for five years, plus an abundant supply of colours, I will do

RUPE RUPE – PICKING FRUIT. 1899.
Hermitage Museum, Leningrad.

anything I am asked, I will paint with a full brush, which takes three times as long.'

With his experience in painting, Gauguin was preoccupied with the preservation of his canvases, and anticipated their internal chemical changes. He was aware of the dangers of applying paint thickly without taking precautions, and he had also noticed that thin paintings, where the paint had not been thickly laid on, aged well and sometimes even improved over the years. 'Now I am not sure, whether in a few years' time when the surface has hardened sufficiently, and the oil has disappeared, you may not find a rich texture, for I remember several canvases, among them a Breton seascape, painted as lightly as possible, which Van Gogh sold to Manzi. After a few years it had become unrecognizable with a very rich surface!' But he did not lose sight of the essential: 'The great thing which is always on

LANDSCAPE WITH THREE TREES. 1892 (?)
Mrs Arthur Lehman Collection.

my mind, is to know whether I am on the right track, whether I am
making progress, or whether I am making mistakes in art. For technical questions, and care in the actual execution, and even the preparation of the canvas are altogether secondary matters. After all,
they can always be remedied, can't they?'

Gauguin was to get the 2,400 francs a year of which he was
dreaming, and they were to come from Vollard, the shameless man,
against whom Gauguin was so prejudiced.

At the beginning of 1900 Chaudet died without having paid Gauguin what he owed him. Vollard suggested to Monfreid that he would
be willing to support Gauguin. At this Gauguin bombarded his friend
with instructions. He was apprehensive of being tied by a contract to
such a dealer! He wanted to discuss his conditions, particularly since
he had learned from Maurice Denis that a few paintings sold at the

Hotel Drouot had fetched far higher prices than he was accustomed to getting. The negotiations were lengthy and laborious. Finally, Vollard accepted all his conditions: he would send Gauguin 300 francs a month, and provide the necessary supplies of paint, canvas and frames; he would pay 200 francs apiece for paintings and 30 francs for drawings. This contract was to transform Gauguin's existence, though he was still suspicious of it. Why should such an experienced businessman take an interest in his painting, at a time when it was generally held that his work did not sell, or only with great difficulty? Nevertheless Gauguin wrote to Vollard to '. . . assure you (you have my word as an artist as a guarantee) that I shall send you nothing that is not Art, and I shall not let you have anything that is mere merchandise, done to earn money. OTHERWISE IT IS USELESS TO SPEAK OF IT ANY FURTHER.' And he went on to define his position: 'I am 51 years old and have one of the greatest reputations in France as well as abroad.' This was addressed to Vollard: '. . . having begun to paint only late in life, there are very few paintings of mine in existence . . . Thus there is no fear of continually having to buy back countless numbers of paintings, as in the case of other artists . . . I put the number of my canvases since I started painting at three hundred at the most. About a hundred of these do not count, since they date from the beginning . . . As you see, this is a very small number. And this should be borne in mind all the more since two hundred francs per painting is the price for a beginner, and not for a man with a well-established reputation.' Sixty years has altered nothing in the business of selling paintings!

Gauguin was now going through a lucky period. An unknown person had sent him 150 francs in advance for a small canvas. He casually mentioned the name of this unusual client to Monfreid: Monsieur Emmanuel Bibesco, 69 rue de Courcelles. This collector was to buy five canvases at 150 francs each. The first was bought immediately, and shortly after, when he learned of the agreement with Vollard, he suggested that he should take the place of the dealer, offering Gauguin an increased rate of 50 francs more for each painting. Gauguin, who did not know the Rumanian prince, was on the defensive. Loyalty prevented him from breaking a contract, which admittedly had no time clause, but had only just been made. He kept Bibesco's proposition as a lever in his dealings with Vollard, and as a possible last resort.

Monsieur Fayet, a collector from Béziers in the south of France, and a rich wine-grower, bought two large paintings. He already possessed some Cézannes and Van Goghs, and he was keeper of the town museum. He sent Gauguin the 1,200 francs shortly afterwards, and asked him for some wood sculptures. The artist had every need of this sum. At the beginning of 1901 he was back in hospital. Both his legs had been covered with purulent sores for months, and left unattended they had become so bad that they prevented him from walking. This setback aggravated Gauguin, and he was afraid of being unable to meet his commitments to Vollard, whom he had promised twenty-five canvases a year.

With his mind at least freed of money worries, Gauguin now discovered that he had exhausted the possibilities of Tahiti; it no longer provided him with inspiration! In April 1901 bubonic plague had broken out in San Francisco and forced all shipping into quarantine, so that the price of merchandise almost tripled. The economic situation looked like getting worse. 'In order to avoid the worst, I am quickly gathering up all I have and although I am very fond of my place here, I am going to try and sell up everything without too much of a loss. Then I shall go and settle on one of the Marquesas Islands, where life is very simple and very cheap. It will mean a loss of time, but basically it will be a good move; my arrangement with Vollard will largely cover the costs, and there I shall find new features to inspire my painting.'

LIFE ON HIVA OA

Certainly, nothing ever proved to be straightforward for Gauguin. He had found a purchaser for his house at Punauia for 5,000 francs. But when it came to signing the deed of sale, the lawyer discovered that Gauguin was married in Europe, and what was worse, under

THE ENCHANTER OR THE SORCERER OF HIVA OA. 1902.
Musée des Beaux-Arts, Liège.

the law of joint estate. This meant he needed an authorization from his wife. Gauguin immediately wrote to Daniel de Monfreid asking him to obtain the legal document from Mette, and informed him of his real reasons for moving to the Marquesas—not only the cost of living, which was always a primary consideration with him, but also 'the ease with which you can find models (something which is becoming more and more difficult in Tahiti) . . .' Now model meant woman. It was this that gave rise to the rumour that Gauguin had become too well known in Tahiti, and could no longer find young Tahitian girls, for whom he had always displayed an excessive predilection. It was said he was leaving in order to find himself girls who were hardly more than children.

The third reason Gauguin had put forward was: 'With undiscovered landscapes, and entirely new and far more wild scenery, I shall be able to do some fine things. Here my imagination was beginning to flag, and then the public was getting too accustomed to Tahiti. Such is the stupidity of people, that if I show them canvases containing new and terrible features, Tahiti will then become comprehensible and charming by comparison. My pictures of Brittany turned into milk-and-water composition in comparison with Tahiti, and the Tahiti ones will be the same in comparison with the Marquesas Isles.' Gauguin completed two carved panels, entitled *War and Peace*, in response to the request of Fayet, who had become one of his most faithful collectors, and he asked to be paid with all speed. He was aiming to build up a sufficiently substantial bank account, to be able to put fresh conditions to Vollard without running any risks, and obtain a revision of their agreement. He could not bear the thought that the dealer was making a fortune at his expense!

His joy at departure made him overlook a number of disappointments, such as the, in his view, untimely publication of *Noa Noa* by Morice. He acknowledged receipt of a hundred copies, describing them as so much 'waste paper'. On the other hand, he showed his appreciation for the initiative this same friend had taken in opening a public subscription fund in order to offer *Where do we come from* to the Museum of Luxembourg. In this case he would have been satisfied to accept 5,000 francs. A few months later Vollard was to pay him 1,500 francs for it! Gauguin was convinced that Vollard never paid for a painting until he had found a prospective buyer.

Without waiting for Mette's authorization, which in fact never came, Gauguin had meanwhile found a way of legally registering the sale of his property at Punauia. It had been sufficient for him to produce the mortgage. Since nothing had appeared from his wife, there was now nothing to prevent the deed of sale being legally passed. The sale brought him 4,500 francs, from which he deducted 800 francs in order finally to pay off the loan from the Agricultural Bank.

He immediately set sail for Atuona on the island of Hiva Oa, a large volcanic reef, barely twenty-five miles across.

STILL LIFE WITH APPLES. 1902 (?)
Basil P. Goulandris Collection, New York.

AND THE GOLD OF THEIR BODIES. 1901.
Louvre, Paris.

There was no land for sale, since everything belonged to the Catholic mission, and Gauguin had to approach Monsignor Martin in order to be granted an assignment of a piece of land. The way in which he had to pay court to the priest was most distasteful to Gauguin, and he took his revenge by making him the butt of his own mockery and attacks. Later he carved caricatures of the bishop and his mistress, calling them *Father Dissolute and Sister Saint Theresa* and placing them in his garden for all the population to see!

Gauguin built a solidly-made house, of which he was very proud. He had sent for wood from Tahiti and a neighbour, Tioka, helped him. The house consisted of a huge studio and one room, raised on piles. He had planned the interior with an eye to his own comfort and provided cool corners, sheltered from the sun, in which to take his siesta. He even had a well dug. The absinth was kept in this, permanently hanging from a long pole, so that he could reach it from the studio without having to move. Gauguin called this house of his dreams 'the house of joy', just as he had once written 'Te Faruru' on the door of his studio in rue Vercingetorix. Now, as then, he was not short of money, but the recriminatory letters did not cease to flow for all that.

So much has been written and rumoured that is entirely false about Gauguin's financial situation that it would be as well to draw up an account of his income during this last stay in the South Seas. Henri Perruchot did in fact do this with scientific accuracy and the figures he assembled are revealing. Gauguin's income from 1895 to January 1900 amounted to 9,036 francs, in addition to which there were his salary earned with the Survey of Papeete, his articles in *Les Guêpes*, and the proceeds of the sale of some copra, the total being less than 10,000 francs. From this must be deducted the cost of the construction of both houses and the interest on the loan from the Agricultural Bank of Papeete – 1,000 francs at least. Thus Gauguin lived on an average of 140 francs per month, which is approximately equivalent to 375 NF, or £27, today.

While we are on the subject of figures, let us anticipate his budget from May 1900, the date of Vollard's first payment, until his death: the total came to 15,220 francs, that is 422 francs per month (approximately 1,000 NF, or £72, today). Even if Vollard did step in at the most advantageous time, and even if Fayet and Monfreid also contributed to the improvement in the artist's circumstances, there is no denying that the dealer's arrangement was also profitable for Gauguin. It is only to be regretted that he did not see fit to display his goodwill earlier.

Now that he was almost entirely relieved of financial worries, Gauguin launched into fresh polemics against the island authorities, and ardently adopted causes that, though admittedly important,

STILL LIFE AND HOPE. 1901.
Nr Nathan Cummings Collection, Chicago, U.S.A.

were only of local interest, compared with his painting. These minor activities led to the neglect and ultimate loss of his health and life.

When he arrived in 1901 he discovered that the inhabitants were not as primitive as they appeared, despite their terrible tattoo marks and their reputation for cannibalism. They were gentle and timorous creatures, terrorized by the two ruling powers, namely the priest and the gendarme. Weakened by the ravages of alcohol and syphilis, they did not dare to protest against the extortions of the Europeans, and their one aim was to keep out of trouble. Gauguin was scandalized by the abuses of power and by the passivity of the natives. For his part, he refused to allow himself to be treated in this way, and his first act of rebellion was to refuse to pay the taxes.

This strange man, clad in a vest and grass-skirt, with a student's green beret on his head, and his swollen, frightful-looking legs, who went about supported by a stick he had carved himself, was to play the part of a Don Quixote and become a legendary figure. The natives' friendly name for him in their dialect was 'Ko Ké'.

He had an ample store of rum, and he had given up eating native food in favour of preserves. The only food he bought on the island was milk and fresh meat, either fowl or pork. Apart from his official mistress, Marie-Rose Vaeoho, who had stopped attending the convent school, there was a steady stream of native girls, one-day models, passing through the 'House of Joy'. They would sometimes be accompanied by men, never Europeans and they would all sing, dance and make merry. This was known throughout Atuona, and the newcomer was the cause of great scandal.

But Gauguin cared nothing for this, or for anything else. He wanted to live and to work. As a matter of fact this way of life agreed with him. He had started painting again with enthusiasm in order to fulfil his commitments to Vollard, but also because he was driven by an inherent need to express in material terms the new emotions aroused in him by the island. He painted flowers and still-life canvases, but the most significant picture from this time is of the two nudes, *And the Gold of their Bodies* (page 247). The nobility and the freshness which he was able to confer on the flesh of these two Marquesan girls make us too feel profoundly the wonder that took possession of him. Once one can share his feelings, it is possible to pardon all his excesses, the way in which he indulged his coarsest instincts, and his worship of primitive animalism.

But this animalism was counterbalanced and offset by a spirituality that was tinged with mysticism. Mystery appealed to him, whether it was concerned with human origins or whether it was the mystery that every human being has buried deep down inside him.

Thus the chance visit of an old blind woman, which had somehow troubled him, inspired him to paint that most enigmatic of canvases, *The Apparition.* The same deliberately disturbing figure appears in *The Call.* What is it that one of these women, with a very grave expression, is bidding the other to do? We shall never know, since Gauguin no longer commented on his canvases, as he had until quite recently, for the benefit of his friends. He now kept the mystery that hovered over his creations to himself. They were bought in advance by Vollard, and Gauguin was not interested in making it easier for him to sell them by supplying anecdotal commentaries.

He was sending canvases back to Europe fairly regularly. Sometimes when the monthly payments were late in arriving he would be seized with anxiety: 'Will he be displeased with the last batch I sent him? All the same, although they are not masterpieces, they are certainly worth every penny he is paying me for them.'

Gauguin was given to assessing and restating issues, and felt the need to put facts and ideas in their proper place. Already certain of his letters were minor philosophic testaments. Referring to Daniel de Monfreid's exhibition at Béziers, he said: 'How right you are to regard praise from the press in this way! First and foremost your own conscience, and then the esteem of the select few, the aristocrats that understand – apart from that nothing else counts!'

'You know what I think of all these false symbolist and other ideas on painting; there is little point in repeating them, as we are both agreed on this subject anyway – as is posterity – since sound works will always survive, and all the critical-literary lucubrations in the world have been unable to change this ...

'I also feel bound to oppose all these groups that are continually setting themselves up to propound various dogmas, and succeed in confusing not only the artist, but worse still the art-loving public.'

His attention also turned to himself, to his past, to the impression he would leave, and the behaviour of his wife: 'I believe a father in prison would have been better treated ... If I am famous after my death, they will say: Gauguin had a large family, he was a patriarch – how ridiculous. Or even: He was a man without guts,

HORSEMEN ON THE BEACH. 1902.
Folkwang Museum, Essen.

who abandoned his children ... Who cares! Let's leave these rotten
bourgeois where they belong—even if they are our own children—
and continue with the work we have begun.'

He was doing a great deal of writing during the year 1902. He
returned to his study on religious issues, altering the title to *Modern
Times and Christianity*. His *Reflections of a Dauber* was a mixture
of studio recollections and aesthetic issues. He recalled the main
episodes in his life, occasionally somewhat embroidered, and tried

PORTRAIT OF THE ARTIST. c. 1903.

to find its moral in *Avant et Après*; this contained an indictment
of Denmark and the Danes, reflections on fencing, memories of personalities he had known from Degas to Bernard, by way of Van
Gogh, a lampoon against colonial administration, and recollections
old and new, all written in a lively, biting and racy style. He sent
the manuscript of *Avant et Après* to André Fontainas, urging him
to get it published at all costs ... which proved impossible. In this
text we find an account of the terrifying hurricane in January 1903,

which caused 515 deaths throughout the archipelago. 'Alone in my house, every moment expecting to see it come crashing down . . . The gusts of wind were pulling at the thin roof, made of leaves of coco-nut-palm . . . My house in ruins, with all my drawings, and posses-sions of twenty years, this would have been disastrous.'

Gauguin had become more preoccupied with his eczema, and the sufferings 'which prevent me from working steadily – for three months I have not touched a brush.' . . . 'Apart from this, I am seriously concerned about my eyesight.' In one of his last portraits, a quick, pencil drawing, he looks like an aged man. His hair is thin with the scalp showing through, and the features are drawn; there are two embittered folds going down on either side of the moustache, which hides the mouth. One can almost guess the folds furrowing the skin, and the look in his eyes appears vacant, without the steel glasses he used for reading, writing and drawing.

Despairing of every kind of treatment, he thought of returning to Europe, believing that the change of air might rid him of the sores that were eating into his legs.

But Daniel de Monfreid saw the situation in another light: 'At present you are known as this extraordinary legendary artist, who from the depths of the South Sea Islands sends his disconcerting and inimitable works, the final works of a great man, who has, as it were, disappeared from the world. Your enemies (and you, like all those who displace mediocrities, have many) say nothing, they dare not oppose you, they do not even think of it . . . In short, you enjoy the immunity of great men who are dead, you have already taken your place in the history of art. The public is learning, and your reputation is steadily growing. Vollard himself is gradually working towards this end. Perhaps he already suspects that you will be in-disputably and universally famous.'

This prophecy of Monfreid's was shortly fulfilled – only posthum-ously. Gauguin was approaching his goal, but he would not have time to enjoy his success. He replied plaintively that he could come to Paris and not show himself there, and go straight on to Spain, so that no one would know he had been in France. He was already dreaming of new themes for his painting. 'Bulls and Spaniards, with their hair plastered down with lard, all that has already been done and overdone – and yet it is strange, I see them in a different way.'

When he had refused to pay his personal tax assessment and dues, Gauguin had written to the administrator of the Marquesas Islands, Monsieur de Saint-Brisson, justifying his attitude by pointing out the shortcomings of the public services. The latter only referred the matter to the higher authorities.

Gauguin attacked the administration on other grounds. He was well-informed: he often met a former sergeant in the marines, named Guilletoue, who had farmed on the island for twenty years, and who was a persistent litigant. With all that he had learned from Guilletoue, Gauguin was to provoke the brigadier of the gendarmerie, Charpillet, to a state of exasperation. He also exploited the existing conflict between the Catholic mission and the Protestant school, which was run by a young pastor by the name of Paul-Louis Vernier. The bishop, Monsignor Martin, retaliated by forbidding his flock to associate with the artist, whose morals he condemned. Gauguin's answer was to make off with the prelate's second housekeeper. These events delighted the natives, and the prelate sensed that his prestige was at stake. Brigadier Charpillet was made to intervene. He did so with obvious reluctance and put up a charge against Gauguin for not having a light on his carriage!

Gauguin ceased to protest on his own behalf, and now turned to action, inciting the natives not to pay their taxes and to stop sending their children to the mission school. His advice was taken. The new governor of the Marquesas received one report after another denouncing the activities of the 'anarchist' artist.

The Taxation Authorities stood firm and Charpillet was ordered to seize and sell the artist's belongings to the amount owing. Gauguin, having held the police-officer up to ridicule, paid the 65 francs that was being claimed.

BARBARIC TALES. 1902.
Folkwang Museum, Essen.

In October 1902 the Governor of the French Possessions in the South Seas made a tour of inspection on board a gunboat. Gauguin seized the opportunity to send him a lampoon in which he denounced the abuses committed by the administration, and sent the text to the *Mercure de France,* which incidentally did not publish it. The governor took no notice of his action.

When a new police-officer, Jean-Pierre Claverie, came to take Charpillet's place, Gauguin accused him of not being sufficiently

ADAM AND EVE. 1902.
Ordrupgaard Museum.

diligent in his enquiry into a crime that had just been committed,
and also accused him of cowardice.

Finally, when two American whaling vessels called at the island
to land contraband merchandise, Gauguin brought a charge. There
is some inconsistency in calling for duty to be paid, when he himself had refused to pay taxes in different circumstances, but Gauguin
was prepared to seize any opportunity to discomfit the gendarmerie.
However, the American boats paid the dues, and Gauguin who had

257

been unaware of this, was unable to withdraw the charges in time. It was this charge together with the accompanying letter that the police-officer, Claverie, used in order to prosecute Gauguin for defamation, following a fresh altercation. Gauguin who regularly attended the court sessions, although he was once again spitting blood, and would interrupt incessantly until he was thrown out, failed to appear when his own case came up. Taken unawares, he had not had the time to consult a Papeete lawyer or warn his friends in Paris. As a result, he was sentenced to three months' imprisonment with a stay of execution, and a fine of 500 francs.

This time the police-officer and the bishop thought they had rid themselves of this fanatical agitator and malcontent, who had come to upset the order and tranquility of the island, and above all who challenged the system which provided them with such a comfortable life. Gauguin had been sent to coventry by the natives, who were afraid of getting involved by being seen with him, and the artist now thought of nothing but completing his life's work. But he wrote to Paris and informed the Governor of his intention to appeal.

It was nevertheless a severe blow, a real 'trap', he called it. He was now faced either with going to the considerable expense of an appeal or paying the fine. And Vollard was once again behind with his monthly payment. Gauguin owed the Société Commerciale 1,400 francs. He was afraid that Vollard was either dead or bankrupt. 'This spells my ruin and the utter destruction of my health. It will be said of me that all my life I was condemned to fall, then pick myself up again, only to fall again, etc. . . . All my former energy is disappearing day by day . . .' And he ended the letter with the ominous words: 'All these anxieties are killing me.'

This was the last news that Europe was to hear from him.

On 23rd August 1903, Daniel de Monfreid received a note from the Administrator of the Marquesas Isles, F. V. Picquenot, worded as follows: 'In fulfilment of my position, among other duties here, as trustee of vacant successions, I believe it my duty to inform you, in view of your friendship with Paul Gauguin, that the death of this artist occurred suddenly on May 9th (sic) last. Yours, etc. . . .'

As soon as he heard of Gauguin's death. Daniel de Monfreid began to collect evidence about his friend's last hours. Pastor Paul-Louis Vernier, who was the last to see Gauguin alive, sent him a long reply, and it is his account that every biography of the painter has drawn upon. Thus we cannot do better than reproduce this letter, whose tone of restrained emotion gives it a special quality.

'I am quite willing to give you some details about the last days of Monsieur Paul Gauguin, and about his death, especially since I looked after him up to the morning of his death, which occurred on 8th May, a Friday, just before eleven o'clock in the morning. Even if I was not his friend – really I hardly knew him, for Gauguin was a wild person – I was his neighbour, and knew about his life. He came to see me on a number of occasions, and three times called me in for a consultation, since I have some medical qualifications.

'In all the time I knew him Monsieur Gauguin was ill and almost impotent. He very rarely left his house, and on the rare occasions when one saw him in the Atuana valley, he made a distressing sight dragging along with difficulty, his legs wrapped in bandages and in his very eccentric attire, looking just like a Maori: a coloured loin-cloth, and the torso clad in the Tahitian vest, nearly always bare-foot, and with his student's beret of green cloth, with a silver buckle on the side. He was a very kind man, very gentle and straightforward to the Marquesans. They returned this in good measure. And after your friend's death, I heard many of the natives utter exclamations of grief, such as: 'Gauguin is dead, we are lost! – *Ua maté Gauguin, ua pété énata!* by which they referred to the way in which Gauguin had often helped them, by rescuing them from the hands of the police, who are often hard and unjust in the case of the natives. In his generous and gallant way, Gauguin had championed the cause of the native. There are numerous instances of his goodness on their behalf.

'He had very little contact with the Europeans of Atuana. I believe he heartily despised them, apart from a few rare exceptions. Above all he detested the police and the law in general. On one occasion

PORTRAIT OF THE ARTIST BY HIMSELF. C. 1903.

(two or three months before his death) he was sentenced to fifteen days in prison and a 500 francs fine on a charge of slandering the police. But Gauguin was convinced he would be acquitted if he appealed. Nevertheless he was preparing to leave for Tahiti when death overtook him. Gauguin appeared to have law and justice on his side, but then anyway he was above all that.'

Pasteur P.-L. Vernier thus substantiates Gauguin's letters, and shows that his prestige was far greater than he had thought.

LANDSCAPE WITH HORSE AND PIG. 1903.
Atheneum Museum, Helsinki.

'As for the countryside, it delighted him and he worshipped the scenery that was so beautiful and so wild, where his soul felt naturally and completely at ease. He immediately discovered the characteristic poetry of these regions blessed by sunshine and as yet untouched by civilization. You must have sensed this from the pictures that he sent back to you. The Maori soul no longer held any mystery for him. Gauguin did, however, feel that our islands were day by day losing some of their distinctiveness.

'"The gods are dead and Atuana is dying from their death," he wrote somewhere . . .

'Towards the beginning of April, I received one morning the following note from Monsieur Gauguin.

'"Dear Monsieur Vernier,

"Would it be troubling you to ask you to come and see me? My eyesight has become very much worse. I am very ill, and I can no longer walk.   P. G."

'I went to see the artist immediately. His legs were giving him dreadful pain, they were red and swollen, and covered in eczema. I suggested the appropriate treatment, offering to dress the affected areas, if he wished. He thanked me very pleasantly, but said he would do it himself. We chatted. Forgetting his pain, he spoke to me of his art in glowing terms, claiming to be an unrecognized genius. He made several references to his altercations with the police, and mentioned several of his friends, though to be honest, I do not recall having heard your name. He lent me several books by Dolent, Aurier, and *L'Après-Midi d'un Faune*, which had been given to him by Mallarmé himself. He gave me a sketched portrait of the latter, bearing the words: *"To monsieur Vernier, a thing of art, P. G."*

'I left him, and did not see him again for ten days. Then old Tioka, Gauguin's friend, came to me saying: "You know, things looks bad with the white man, he is very ill!" I went back to see your friend, and found him very low indeed, lying stretched out and groaning. Again he forgot his pain to talk of art. I admired his devotion to it.

'On the morning of 8th May, he had this same Tioka call me. I went there. Gauguin was still in bed, and complained of severe pains in his body. He asked me if it was morning or evening. He told me he had fainted twice, and he was worried about this. He spoke to me of *Salammbô*. When I left him, he was lying on his back, calm and relaxed, after these few minutes' conversation. Towards eleven o'clock that morning, young Ka Hui, the servant (all too casual, unfortunately, in the sense that he would often leave his master's house while he was ill) came running agitatedly to call me, saying: "Come quickly, the white man has died!"

'I flew there. I found Gauguin lying lifeless, with one leg hanging out of the bed, but he was still warm. Tioka was there, beside himself. "I came to see how he was, and called up Ko Ké from below (Ko Ké was the natives' name for Gauguin). Hearing nothing, I climbed up to see. Oh, Oh! Gauguin did not stir. He was dead," he said, and so saying, he bit right into his friend's scalp, which is a Marquesan way of trying to restore someone to life. I myself tried rhythmical traction on the tongue, and artificial respiration, but nothing worked. Paul Gauguin really was dead, and everything indicated that he had a sudden heart failure.

'I am the last European to have seen Gauguin before he died. I must say that he never spoke to me of his family in Europe, nor did he give me any instructions, and he did not say anything about his last wishes. His papers were gone through by the authorities, and I believe that they found nothing. There was a rumour that he had a family in Europe, a wife and five children. There was a photograph in his hut of a family group, which was said to be of them. I saw the photograph. There were other rumours, quite apart from that. One didn't know what to believe. Naturally, I never asked Gauguin about this. I ought to say a few words now about the circumstances under which he was buried.' (This gave rise to heated arguments, since religious issues were still a source of bitter conflict in the Marquesas.)

'When I reached Gauguin, on that fateful Friday, after I had been told of his death, I found the Catholic priest of the Marquesas and several monks already seated at his bedside. I was absolutely astounded to see them there. Gauguin's feelings towards *these gentlemen* were common knowledge, and *these gentlemen* were only too well aware

BRETON VILLAGE IN THE SNOW. 1894 (?)
Louvre, Paris.

of them. My astonishment turned to indignation when I learned that Monsieur the Bishop had decided to bury Gauguin according to full Catholic ritual, and this took place on Saturday 9th May. It had been arranged that the funeral should start from the house at two o'clock. I wanted to be present at least when the procession started out, and accordingly I went to Gauguin's house at the appointed time. His body had been taken to the church one hour and a half before. As you see, this was a deliberate piece of deception. And Gauguin now lies in the Roman Catholic cemetery, holy land if ever there was! In my opinion, Gauguin should have had a secular burial.

'There were two auction sales of Gauguin's possessions. The first was held in Atuana itself, and here the things likely to be bought by the natives and the few Europeans in the place were sold – his clothing, trunks, carpentry and woodwork tools, his cooking equipment and stove, his horse, his preserves, and wine, his house and the ground (in one single lot) which went I believe, to an American businessman for 1,050 francs. The green beret fell to Tioka, who wore it night and day, it had been given to him by the auctioneer. Poor Gauguin!

'The second sale took place in Tahiti and consisted solely of things of value, paintings in particular, and rare objects. Doctor Segalen has informed you about this . . .'

Victor Segalen, medical officer on board the ship 'La Durance' which had been cruising in the South Seas related what he had been able to see, in the 'Tribute to Gauguin' which formed the introduction to the published collection of Gauguin's letters to Daniel de Monfreid. He visited the 'House of Joy'. In a dark corner he came upon the statuette of baked clay representing 'a Buddha born on Maori soil', which had caused Gauguin to be accused of paganism. It was so cracked and fragile that he did not dare to subject it to the hazards of a sea journey and preferred to leave it to crumble into dust on the spot where Gauguin had put it. He received confirmation of the facts we have reported here both from the natives and from the police and the missionary. Finally, he attended the sale of so-called 'valuable' objects in Papeete. The public consisted of dealers, officials and a few naval officers like himself. An album of drawings was bought on behalf of the governor. A pearl dealer by the name of Levy wanted the stick decorated with a huge inset pearl and the two wood carvings of *Father Dissolute and Sister Saint Theresa*, which had unleashed the wrath of the caricatured prelate. A drawing teacher acquired all Gauguin's artist materials for 3 francs, and a naval officer went up to 150 francs for a work called *Motherhood*. As for Segalen, he bought the artist's palette for 40 sous, which he gave to Daniel de Monfreid, and he bought the wood carvings which had decorated the 'House of Joy' for 16 francs, and not, as he wrote, 100, and for 87 francs, seven paintings, including the *Self-Portrait at Golgotha*. One canvas was displayed upside-down by the auctioneer under the title of 'Niagara Falls' to the great hilarity of those present, and fell to Segalen for 7 francs. This was a Breton snow-covered landscape and its presence on Gauguin's easel at the time of his death is enigmatic (page 264). Victor Segalen thought that in his nostalgia for Europe it was the last work to have come from the hand of the artist. However it might well have been one of the pictures Gauguin had brought back from Europe with him.

As for the manuscript of *Noa Noa* and the other personal papers that were not destroyed, these were sent back to Europe thanks to the Ministry for Colonies, and conveyed to Daniel de Monfreid, whom Mette had appointed as her husband's executor.

After the posthumous sales, there remained 4,151 francs to Gauguin's credit in Tahiti. This Daniel de Monfreid sent to Mette Gauguin, together with the proceeds from the sale of a number of other canvases.

In the same year Vollard exhibited about a hundred of his works, and the Autumn Salon arranged a retrospective exhibition of the painter of Tahiti.

Henceforth Gauguin belonged to history and the old quarrels caused by his way of life died out far more quickly than the aesthetic discussions, which his work contined to arouse for a long time. His work also became the object of speculative buying, for the cost of his paintings steadily rose and attained fabulous prices.

Gauguin would certainly have been happy to know of this, but he would have been even more happy to know of the reforms introduced by the Colonial administration in the Marquesas Isles after his death; officials were dismissed and replaced, and disciplinary measures adopted that justified his actions and vindicated him but, as with his painting, unfortunately too late.

LIST OF ILLUSTRATIONS

Numbers shown in italic type denote reproductions in colour

INDEX OF NAMES